The Vintage House Book

Classic American Homes 1880-1980

TAD BURNESS

Published by

700 East State Street • Iola, WI 54990-0001
715-445-2214 • 888-457-2873
www.krause.com

Please call or write for our free catalog of publications. Our toll-free number to place an order or obtain a free catalog is 800-258-0929, or please use our regular business telephone 715-445-2214.

Library of Congress Catalog Number: 2002113142

ISBN: 0-87349-533-0

Acknowledgments

Though I was only able to include a fraction of my picture and reference collection in this volume, I'm grateful to those who, over the past several years, sold to me or freely contributed pictures or information helpful to either this specific book or to my reference collection in general. In alphabetical order, these individuals and organizations include:

Joseph Altieri
Bert Aronson
Associated Brokers
Charles Aucutt

Don Beals
Bill Bluhm
Bonafied Properties
Bratty Real Estate
Robert T. Bratty
Tom Bruce
Burchell House Properties
Buyer's Real Estate

Calandra Real Estate
California Arts and
    Architecture
Carmel Realty Company
Century 21 Real Estate, Scenic
    Bay Properties
Chelew and Campbell (Rose
    Marie Coleman)
Sharon Christensen
Coldwell Banker
Bob Cowan
Herman Smith Curtis

David Real Estate (A.G., Jeff,
    John, et al)
Del Monte Real Estate
Adeline Di Lorenzo
Draper Realty
Wallea Draper

George East

First City Realty
Fouratt-Simmons Real Estate
Richard Fowler

Game and Gossip
Joanne Garden
Terri Gelardi
Bruce Gilbert

Harbor Real Estate
Pat Hathaway
Ben Heinrich Real Estate
Lawrence C. Holian

International Estates

Elliott Kahn

Chuck & Wendy Lazer
Sal Lucido

Jane Mamat
Nancy McCullough
Merit McBride Realty
Mitchell Group
Monterey Board of Realtors
Monterey Peninsula Associates

National Trust for Historic
    Preservation
Nations Estates
Lynda Nichols

Ocean Avenue Realty
John Olkoski

Pacific Bay Realty
Pacific Grove Heritage Society
    (a.k.a. Heritage Society of
    Pacific Grove)
Pacific Grove Real Estate
Pan American Real Estate
    Company

Peninsula Realty
Alain Pinel Realtors
Roy Pohlmann
Porter-Marquard Real Estate
Prestige Properties
Betty Pribula
Marlene Provence
Prudential California Realty

Red Carpet Realty
Remax
Lois Renk & Associates
John Reynolds
Sal Rombi
Deen Rowe
Deane Rudoni

John Saar Properties
San Carlos Agency
John Sansone, Sr.
Saturday Evening Post
Bert Saunders
Larry Scholink
Seven Cities by the Sea
Harry Shaw
Rand Smith
Sunset
Gail Szafran

Herb Towle
Tri-City Real Estate

Marilyn Vassallo
Hank Veloz

Adam Weiland
Windermere Preferred Properties
Carol Winningham

Foreword

by Wendell Nelson

Before the 1976 bicentennial, few Americans seemed to care about preserving old buildings, and few books were published on our architectural history. In 2002, however, many buildings are being restored, preserved, and written about. And many books are available on American buildings, especially old houses: the histories of styles in general, on one or another particular style, and on the old houses of a specific city, state, or region.

The Vintage House Book is a unique addition to this growing body of architectural history, and it is an ambitious book. While whole books are now written on the houses of a small city or on a single style or even a single feature like a cupola or veranda, this one covers nothing less than a whole century of a dozen or more basic styles, with numerous variations and combinations.

But the book is even more than that. It is also a history of American material culture from 1879–1980, including not only our houses, but also our garages, toilets, water heaters, thermostats, kitchen ranges, chairs, building materials, bicycles, cars, hats, and toys. Houses of many social and economic classes are also represented: shanties, cabins, apartment buildings, middle-class houses, local mansions, and grand palaces. A few images even show houses being built and remodeled.

The format of this book is as distinctive as its content. It is not a straightforward history, but a kaleidoscope of hundreds of pieces of information, verbal and visual, scattered around each page and loosely organized chronologically. It reminds one of newspaper cartoons, with each panel having pictures and words, often laid out, seemingly haphazardly, around the space. A Sears, Roebuck or Montgomery Ward catalogue, part illustration and part text, also comes to mind. Those were vintage and quintessentially American popular formats, so this book is in fitting company.

It informs us by impressionism, much as do the paintings of Monet and Seurat. We look around each page, and slowly we absorb and become aware of objects and patterns and themes. And we gradually find ourselves drawn into the world of these vintage houses, as if we were walking down a 1910 street, looking at them: new and old, big and little, simple and ornate. We feel what it was like for, say, a bank teller to look in plan books and catalogues for the design and furnishings of the new house he wants to have built for his family.

As you'll notice, styles did not begin and end abruptly, but gradually merged one into another. One gets a sense of the passage of history in our everyday world. This eclectic slice of American architecture entertains us while leaving us better-informed and more observant of houses and many other features around us.

∽

Wendell Nelson, who also wrote the chapter introductions for this book, is an old-house expert currently living in Portage County, Wisconsin. Nelson has given hundreds of tours, classes, and slide talks on many aspects of the history of Portage County and Central Wisconsin. He is also a consultant on old-house research and restoration. He has published many articles on local history and buildings and has written three books, including *Houses That Grew: Old Houses of Stevens Point, Wisconsin*. He is now writing two more books on the history of Portage County and the houses of its villages and farms.

Nelson received a B.A. in English and history from St. Cloud (Minnesota) State University in 1963, and an M.A. in English from Southern Illinois University in 1966.

Table of Contents

Won't you come in?

Open the pages of *The Vintage House Book*, and tour 102 years of old houses, inside and out, year-by-year, from 1879 to 1980 (the title states "1880 to 1980," but I tossed in a bonus year).

See thousands of houses of all styles, plus rooms, kitchens, bathrooms, basements and attics, appliances, and other features that will help you determine the age of nearly any older house that hasn't been heavily remodeled. If you've never seen the inside of a really old house, here's your chance! Many floor plans are also included!

There are many illustrations, including original advertising of very early plumbing fixtures—weird-looking, primitive ones that are entirely different from what we see today! Many kitchens from bygone years are also featured, with their old-fashioned (and now collectible) appliances.

If you own and plan to restore an old house, this book will be helpful in showing you items you may want to hunt down in order to return the house to its original look. Pages that look at doors, windows, light fixtures and switches, thermostats, and heaters will give you many options.

And, did you know that several companies used to sell "house kits" by mail order so people could assemble these kits on their vacant lots and build their own house, or have it built, at well below the going market price? Everything needed to build a complete house could be ordered and delivered by train or truck in one big package! There were many such providers of kit houses: Sears, Roebuck is the best remembered, offering dozens of different house kits from 1908 to 1940. And there were others, such as Aladdin, Lewis, and Montgomery Ward. Sterling System, Bennett Homes, Pacific Ready-Cut, Gordon-Van Tine, Carey, and Hodgson Houses were sold throughout the U.S.A. They can all be seen in this book!

For an immensely detailed and complete history of Sears, Roebuck kit houses, with pictures and floor plans of all their models, I recommend the book *Houses by Mail*, by Katherine Cole Stevenson and H. Ward Jandl. It's still available, as I write this, from Preservation Press, John Wiley and Sons. It contains valuable information and even names the many cities where certain Sears kit house types were sold and built!

The Vintage House Book is the culmination of decades of detailed research and collecting thousands and thousands of rare pictures, photos, and ads dealing with old houses, appliances, plumbing fixtures, and building materials. This started as a hobby back in the 1960s, as I began collecting all kinds of old pictorial and reference material to build up an eventual "book mine" from which I could harvest irreplaceable material for future non-fiction books.

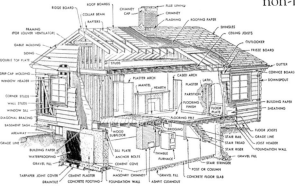

As a boy, I accompanied my parents on many tours of old houses for sale or rent, and my interest grew. I even worked in real estate sales for a brief time, but my real interest was in writing and illustrating. There was a long-unfulfilled need for a book like this, which would span the development of American houses, year by year.

Please notice the beautiful old artwork, exquisitely detailed etchings, in many of the earliest black-and-white ad and catalog illustrations. In the color pages, you will find superb kitchen and bathroom pictures, most of them from rare original advertisements no longer available—not even in libraries or universities, which periodically discard their "obsolete" material!

This book's been a labor of love from the outset, but another labor of love is Michael, Mark & Stevie, a nostalgic family comic feature I've been working on for some time and hope to eventually publish. Included here are two of the many episodes of Michael, Mark & Stevie.

MICHAEL, MARK and STEVIE

MICHAEL, MARK and STEVIE

You're anxious to enjoy everything on all the following pages, and I hope you'll browse through *The Vintage House Book* many times for years to come! Thank you for your kind and lasting interest.

With very best wishes,
Tad Burness
P.O. Box 247
Pacific Grove, CA 93950

Chapter

1 1879-1889

In general, the farther west that the American frontier was settled, the later its buildings were built. This book starts in 1879, relatively late in the history of house styles. The earliest houses in this book are small and simple. A scarcity of both money and materials made large ornate houses a rarity. Some later ones in this decade had some "gingerbread" or ornately carved wood trim on them, but basically they were modest.

Five standard high-style periods constitute the major themes in this decade, which in some ways is the height of the Victorian Period. Gothic Revival, Italianate, and Second Empire (mansard) had been around for some years by 1879, and so were fading in popularity. Stick Style and Queen Anne appeared during these years, and they continued to be popular for several more.

This chapter also introduces a style referred to here as "Early Tudor Revival." The Tudor revival style is generally seen much later in the history of American houses. The "Early Tudor Revival" has the period's typical half-timbered exterior walls and very small-paned oriel windows, but it is a hybrid. It also has such Queen Anne features as porches with arched bays and colonial details like gabled dormers.

Indoor plumbing also makes its debut in the late 1800s. Inventors had been experimenting for many years with various designs for toilets and sinks and showers, but by the 1880s many larger and more expensive houses were plumbed, making the old outhouses obsolete.

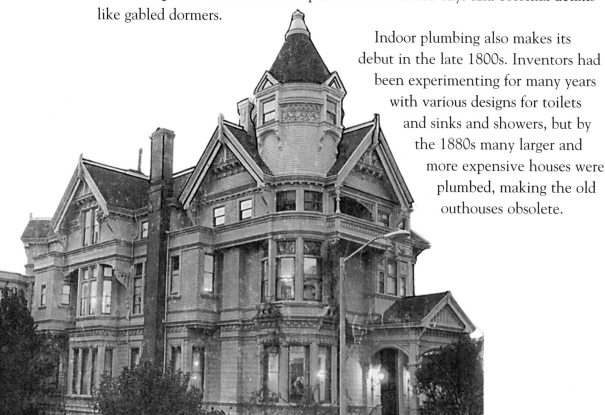

TO RESPECT THE PRIVACY OF CURRENT OWNERS, STREET ADDRESSES OF HOUSES ARE NOT INCLUDED.

remodel

OLDEST HOUSE IN PACIFIC GROVE, CA., BUILT IN 1879* AND SHOWN AS IT APPEARED IN SEPT., 1999 WHEN I TOOK THIS PHOTO. ←

A VERY EARLY, CRUDE PHOTO OF ABOVE HOUSE, AS IT ORIGINALLY APPEARED

1879~ 1880

NOTICE THE EXTREMES IN SIZES AND STYLES OF HOMES!

THOUGH I WASN'T ALLOWED TO ENTER THE TOWER, AS A TEENAGER, I TOURED A HUGE "1882" MANSION, JUST EAST OF EL CAMINO REAL, IN MENLO PARK, CA., IN 1950. IT WAS FOR SALE FOR ONLY $25,000., SINCE LARGE OLD VICTORIANS WERE OF LITTLE VALUE THEN! THIS → MAY BE THAT HOUSE, THOUGH I DON'T RECALL THE TOWER BEING QUITE THIS TALL.

WM. FLOOD MANSION IN MENLO PARK, CA.

CONSTR. BEGAN 1879

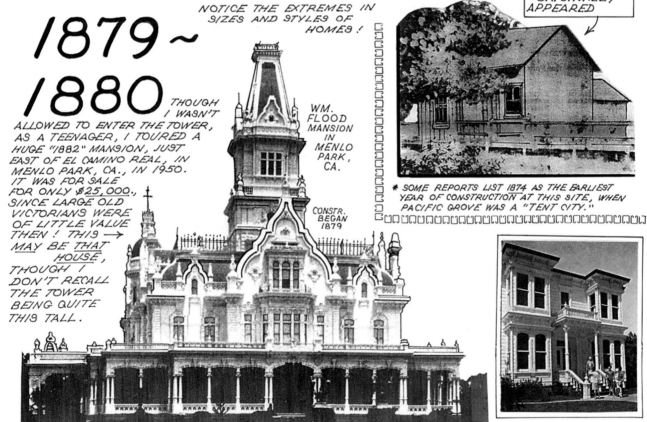

* SOME REPORTS LIST 1874 AS THE EARLIEST YEAR OF CONSTRUCTION AT THIS SITE, WHEN PACIFIC GROVE WAS A "TENT CITY."

PACIFIC GROVE,
CA. 1880

BAT~AND~
BOARD
EXTERIOR

STAINED~
GLASS
ARCHED
WINDOW
BY A
STAIRCASE
LANDING →

(ABOVE) CALIFORNIA FARMHOUSE STYLE

ORNATE HAND~PAINTED WOODWORK ON 1880 MANSION CEILING.

1880

MANSION with CENTRAL TOWER PITTSBURGH,
PA.

1880-81

PACIFIC GROVE,
CA.

TURRET

QUEEN 1880
ANNE
STYLE

SALEM, OH.

1881

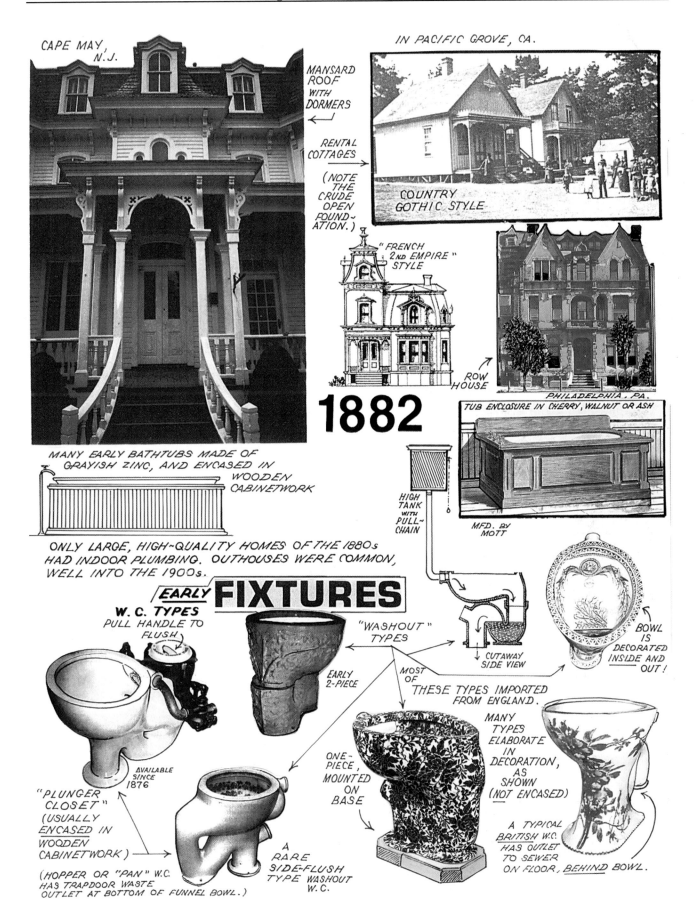

CAPE MAY, N.J.

IN PACIFIC GROVE, CA.

MANSARD ROOF WITH DORMERS ←

RENTAL COTTAGES

(NOTE THE CRUDE OPEN FOUNDATION.)

COUNTRY GOTHIC STYLE

"FRENCH 2ND EMPIRE" STYLE

ROW HOUSE

PHILADELPHIA, PA.

1882

MANY EARLY BATHTUBS MADE OF GRAYISH ZINC, AND ENCASED IN WOODEN CABINETWORK

TUB ENCLOSURE IN CHERRY, WALNUT OR ASH

HIGH TANK WITH PULL-CHAIN

MFD. BY MOTT

ONLY LARGE, HIGH-QUALITY HOMES OF THE 1880s HAD INDOOR PLUMBING. OUTHOUSES WERE COMMON, WELL INTO THE 1900s.

EARLY FIXTURES

W.C. TYPES
PULL HANDLE TO FLUSH

"WASHOUT" TYPES

CUTAWAY SIDE VIEW

BOWL IS DECORATED INSIDE AND OUT!

EARLY 2-PIECE

MOST OF THESE TYPES IMPORTED FROM ENGLAND.

AVAILABLE SINCE 1876

"PLUNGER CLOSET" (USUALLY ENCASED IN WOODEN CABINETWORK) →

(HOPPER OR "PAN" W.C. HAS TRAPDOOR WASTE OUTLET AT BOTTOM OF FUNNEL BOWL.)

ONE-PIECE, MOUNTED ON BASE

A RARE SIDE-FLUSH TYPE WASHOUT W.C.

MANY TYPES ELABORATE IN DECORATION, AS SHOWN (NOT ENCASED)

A TYPICAL BRITISH W.C. HAS OUTLET TO SEWER ON FLOOR, BEHIND BOWL.

HOUSES

COTTAGE WITH VERTICAL
BAT-AND-BOARD SIDING

STRIPED ROOF A
BRIEF FAD

1883

THESE HOUSES LOCATED IN THE
ORIGINAL "RETREAT" DISTRICT OF
PACIFIC GROVE, CA.

BAY WINDOW
ADDITION

GOTHIC VERNACULAR
COTTAGE (ABOVE)
(A.K.A.
"CARPENTER'S
GOTHIC" STYLE)

THE
HORSE~AND~
BUGGY
WAS THE
PRINCIPAL
FORM OF
TRANSPORTATION.

THIS
HOUSE
WAS RAISED,
SO A
7' HIGH
BASEMENT LEVEL COULD BE ADDED.

U.S. CIVIL SERVICE ESTABLISHED

"JEWEL COTTAGE,"
PACIFIC GROVE, CA. (REPLACED 1961
BY A NEW 3~UNIT APT. HOUSE)

TOWER ~ STYLE HOME IN
PACIFIC GROVE, CA.

VICTORIAN
GOTHIC

1883

WESTERN/SOUTHERN
BRICK VICTORIAN with
UPSTAIRS DORMER,
FULL~WIDTH
FRONT
PORCH

SMALL
BAT~AND~BOARD
VERNACULAR
COTTAGE

NOTE
THE
UNUSUAL
WOOD~
AND~WIRE
FENCE !

(BRICK HOUSES USUALLY FOUND in MIDWEST and EAST.)

ENCASED W. C.

EARLY WATER CLOSETS *

HOPPER TYPE

* USUALLY ENCASED IN WOODEN CABINETS

PLEASE NOTE ═ PLUMBING FIXTURES ILLUSTRATED NEAR HOUSES DOES *NOT* IMPLY THAT THOSE FIXTURES WERE *FROM* SAID HOUSES.

1884

WASH STAND
HALF-CIRCLE TYPE

"IMPERIAL" PORCELAIN SEAT BATH

"SLOP SINK" (FOR WASHING MOPS, ETC.)

← ORIGINALLY THE RESIDENCE OF JUDGE BENJAMIN J. LANGFORD, WHO TENDED THE GATE TO ADMIT VISITORS TO PACIFIC GROVE, CA. (ORIGINALLY A METHODIST RETREAT CAMP.) WHEN THE JUDGE GOT TIRED OF THE BUSY ADMISSION GATE, HE CHOPPED IT DOWN! THIS HOUSE IS NOW "THE GATEHOUSE INN."

NOTE ORNATE DECORATIVE "GINGERBREAD"

PORCH WRAPS AROUND 2 SIDES

1884

LARGE "QUEEN ANNE" WITH TOWER AND PORCHES

ITALIANATE INFLUENCE

DECORATIVE
OVAL
WINDOW
(EAST COAST
HOUSE)

TRIPLE WINDOWS

FEW OTHER VICTORIAN
HOUSES WERE AS TALL
AS THIS 5½-STORY
WONDER!

NOTE DECORATIVE HORIZONTAL
WOOD STRIPS ON WALLS
(ABOVE)

1885

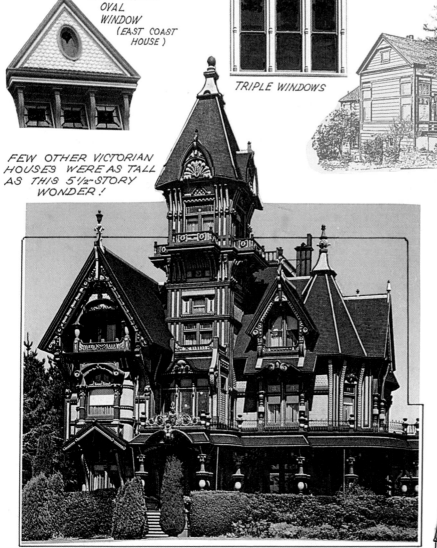

1885 SINGER BICYCLE

CARSON MANSION, EUREKA, CA.
ONE OF THE MOST IMPRESSIVE
VICTORIAN HOMES OF 1885! NOTE THE
HEAVY USE OF "GINGERBREAD"
ORNAMENTATION!

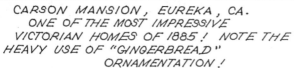

RECENT
VIEW

IMPROVEMENTS MADE SINCE 1885

TRIPLE
WASH
TUBS
WITH
WRINGER

ITALIANATE STYLE (NO, THIS IS **NOT** ADJACENT TO THE NOTORIOUS "BATES MOTEL.")

STAINED GLASS WINDOW →

2 VIEWS OF THE SAME HOUSE

(THIS HOUSE SURVIVED FOR 100 YEARS, UNTIL 1985, BUT WAS THEN TORN DOWN AND REPLACED BY A NEO-VICTORIAN COMMERCIAL STRUCTURE, IN 1986.)

ORNATE WINDOW DETAIL →

1885

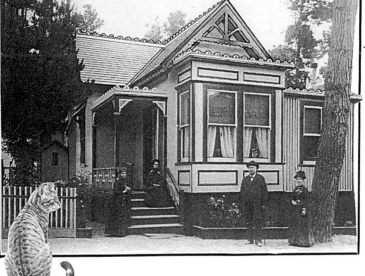

HOUSES IN PACIFIC GROVE, CALIFORNIA

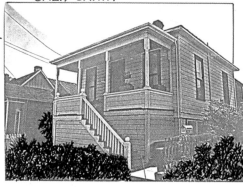

BRIDGEPORT, CT.   DESIGNED BY FRANK D. NICHOLS, BRIDGEPORT, CONN.

27½" LONG
CHILD'S TUB

ORIGINAL 1886
COST OF
THIS HOUSE:
$1800.

FLOOR PLAN

1ST FLOOR   2ND FLOOR

18
86

PANTRY   LOBBY

DINING ROOM   KITCHEN

PARLOR   HALL

PORCH

CLOSET
CLOSET
BED ROOM   BED ROOM
STAIRWAY TO ATTIC
BED ROOM   BATH

WOOD ~
ENCASED
TUB WITH
SHOWER BATH
and
CURTAIN
RING

BOILERS
(HOT
WATER HEATERS) AVAIL. IN
THE FOLLOWING
GALLON CAPACITIES:
18, 21, 24, 27, 28,
30, 32, 35, 36,
40, 42, 47 (ALL OF
GALVANIZED IRON.)*
(OF COPPER:
30, 35, 40,
45, 50, 60,
70, 80, 90,
OR 100
GALLONS)

STAND, FOR HOT WATER
HEATER BOILER

WOOD ~ ENCASED W.C.

BOILER
1886   A

(* CERTAIN GALV. IRON BOILERS UP TO 192 GALS.   SOME SIZES UNAVAIL. UNTIL 1888)

HIGH
WOODEN
TANK

PORCELAIN
BOWL

TEMPLETON, CA.

SINK

TUB

FOOT BATH

1880s BATHROOMS SOMETIMES HAD ALL
PLUMBING FIXTURES ENCASED IN
WOODEN CABINETWORK (ABOVE)

SIDE~WASHOUT IRON~TRAP
TOILET BOWL. THIS TYPE
USUALLY ENCASED IN
WOOD.

TRIPLEX

1886

CUPOLA, A.K.A.
"BELVEDERE"
VIEW ROOM →

CORNER
WASH
BOWL
AND
SLAB

SAN
FRANCISCO,
CA.

MANSION ═ QUEEN ANNE STYLE

SIMPLE, TALL
BOX SHAPE with
DIAGONAL
BAY WINDOW

EARLY PHOTO IN
PACIFIC GROVE, CA.

2~STORY HOUSE AT RIGHT
BUILT 1886

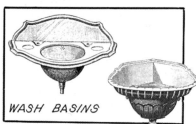

WASH BASINS

HAYWARD, CA.

1886

AUTOMATIC~ACTION W.C.
(SEAT CONNECTED TO
FLUSHING CHAIN)
2½~GALLON FLUSH

BOWL
PARTIALLY
CONCEALED
BY
SEAT
FRAME

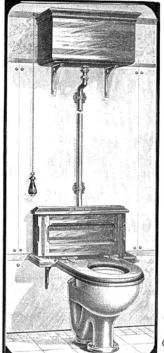

MOTT
FREE~
STANDING
WATER
CLOSET

MEN'S REST ROOM

WITH BAY WINDOW

CORNER
CABINET
LAVATORY

50TH YEAR OF VICTORIA'S REIGN
AS QUEEN OF ENGLAND

1887

FREE-STANDING
ARTISTIC STYLED
BATHTUB

DECORATED
WASH BASINS WERE
SET IN CABINETWORK

BAT-AND-BOARD CONSTRUCTION

BEACH COTTAGE

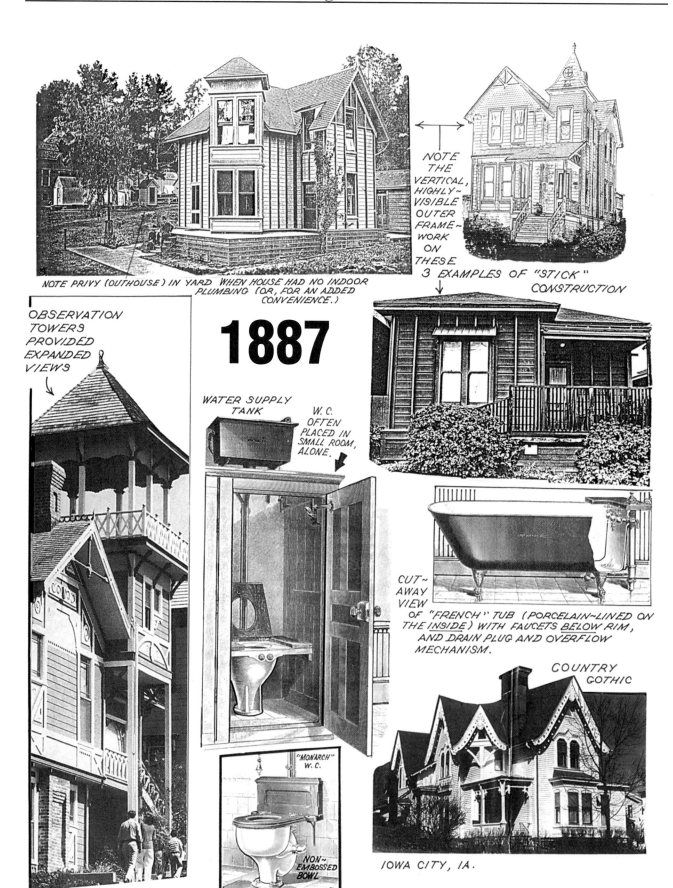

NOTE PRIVY (OUTHOUSE) IN YARD. WHEN HOUSE HAD NO INDOOR PLUMBING (OR, FOR AN ADDED CONVENIENCE.)

NOTE THE VERTICAL, HIGHLY~ VISIBLE OUTER FRAME~ WORK ON THESE 3 EXAMPLES OF "STICK" CONSTRUCTION

1887

OBSERVATION TOWERS PROVIDED EXPANDED VIEWS

WATER SUPPLY TANK

W.C. OFTEN PLACED IN SMALL ROOM, ALONE.

CUT~AWAY VIEW OF "FRENCH" TUB (PORCELAIN~LINED ON THE INSIDE) WITH FAUCETS BELOW RIM, AND DRAIN PLUG AND OVERFLOW MECHANISM.

COUNTRY GOTHIC

"MONARCH" W.C.

NON~EMBOSSED BOWL

IOWA CITY, IA.

ARCATA, CA.

"QUEEN ANNE" STYLE FREQUENTLY INCLUDES TOWERS, TURRETS, AND DECORATIVE "GINGERBREAD" SHINGLED SIDING.
(VARIOUS 1887 QUEEN ANNE EXAMPLES ON THIS PAGE)

EMBOSSED, HAND-PAINTED CEILING (IN HOUSE ILLUSTR. BELOW)

CAREY, OHIO

1887

SAN DIEGO, CA.

NOTE THE STAINED-GLASS WINDOWS

"WITCHES CAP" TOWER ROOF

STAIRWELL DETAILS

OPEN
RECESSED
LAVATORY
SINK =
MARBLE
SLAB
WITH
OVAL
WASH
BASIN →
and
IMPROVED
FAUCETS
(BY
MOTT)

GREEN GABLES INN
PACIFIC GROVE,
CA.

1888

ORIGINAL ↑
COST TO
BUILD THIS
GRAND
QUEEN ANNE
VICTORIAN IN
ALAMEDA, CA.,
IN 1888, WAS
ONLY
$2600.!

NEW
ENGLAND
STYLE

"IMPERIAL" PORCELAIN KITCHEN SINK

SIDE~OUTLET
VALVE
CLOSET
(CABINET
SHOWN AT
FAR LEFT,
IN CHERRY OR
WALNUT/ASH)

CUT-AWAY VIEW

BEACH VICTORIAN

SOME VICTORIAN
HOUSES HAVE
BEEN CONVERTED TO
BUSINESSES.

MONA LISA   MEXICAN

CLOSED

COMMERCIAL PROPERTY

1888

CHILD'S
BATH

FOOT BATHS

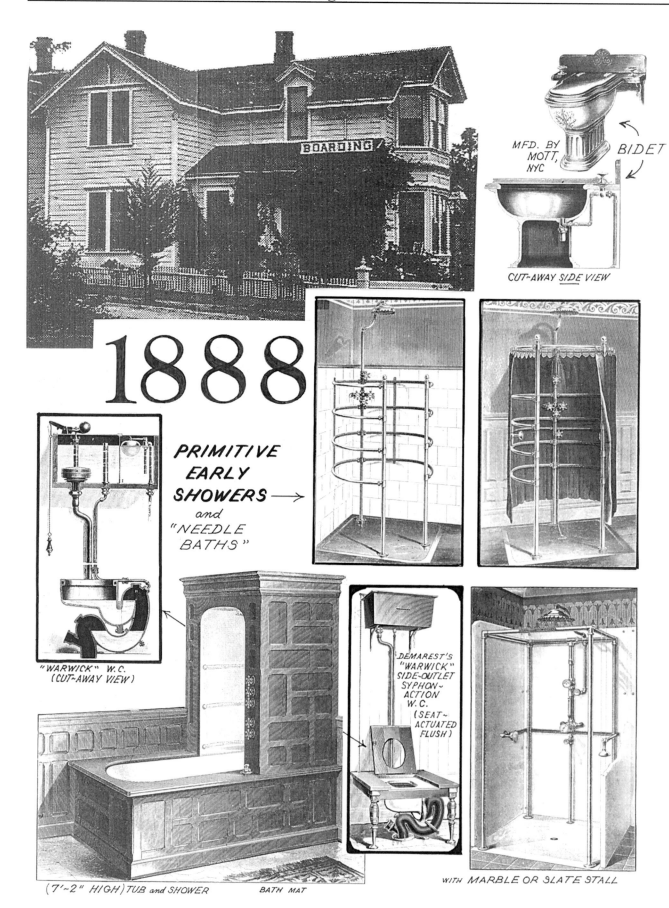

BOARDING

1888

MFD. BY MOTT, NYC

BIDET

CUT-AWAY SIDE VIEW

PRIMITIVE
EARLY
SHOWERS →
and
"NEEDLE
BATHS"

"WARWICK" W.C.
(CUT-AWAY VIEW)

DEMAREST'S
"WARWICK"
SIDE-OUTLET
SYPHON-
ACTION
W.C.
(SEAT-
ACTUATED
FLUSH)

(7'~2" HIGH) TUB and SHOWER   BATH MAT

WITH MARBLE OR SLATE STALL

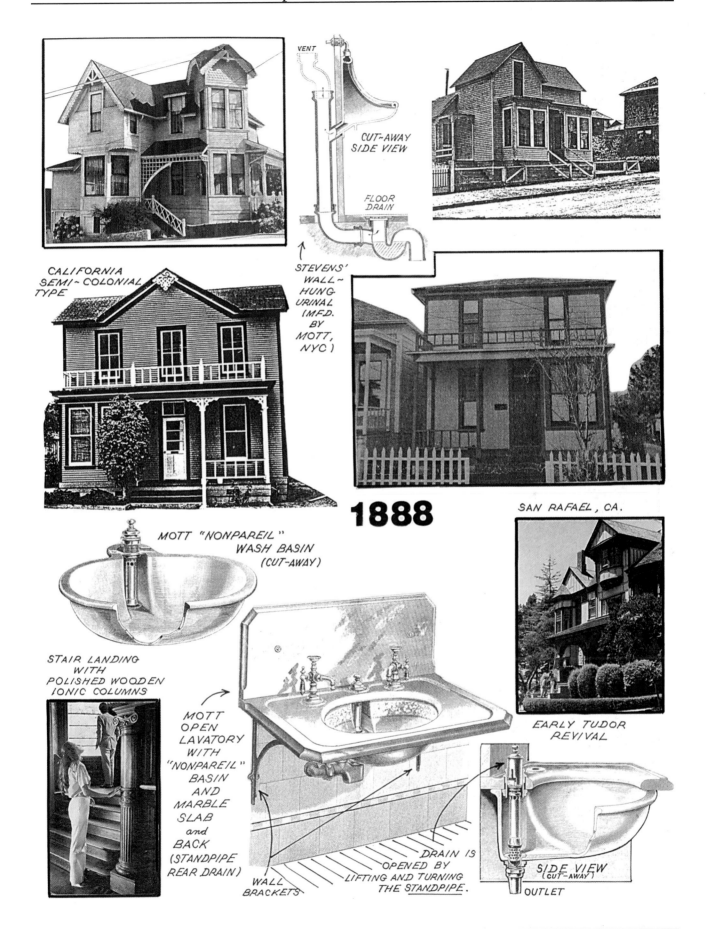

CALIFORNIA SEMI~COLONIAL TYPE

VENT

CUT~AWAY SIDE VIEW

FLOOR DRAIN

STEVENS' WALL~HUNG URINAL (MFD. BY MOTT, NYC)

1888

SAN RAFAEL, CA.

MOTT "NONPAREIL" WASH BASIN (CUT-AWAY)

STAIR LANDING WITH POLISHED WOODEN IONIC COLUMNS

MOTT OPEN LAVATORY WITH "NONPAREIL" BASIN AND MARBLE SLAB and BACK (STANDPIPE REAR DRAIN)

WALL BRACKETS

DRAIN IS OPENED BY LIFTING AND TURNING THE STANDPIPE.

EARLY TUDOR REVIVAL

SIDE VIEW (CUT-AWAY)

OUTLET

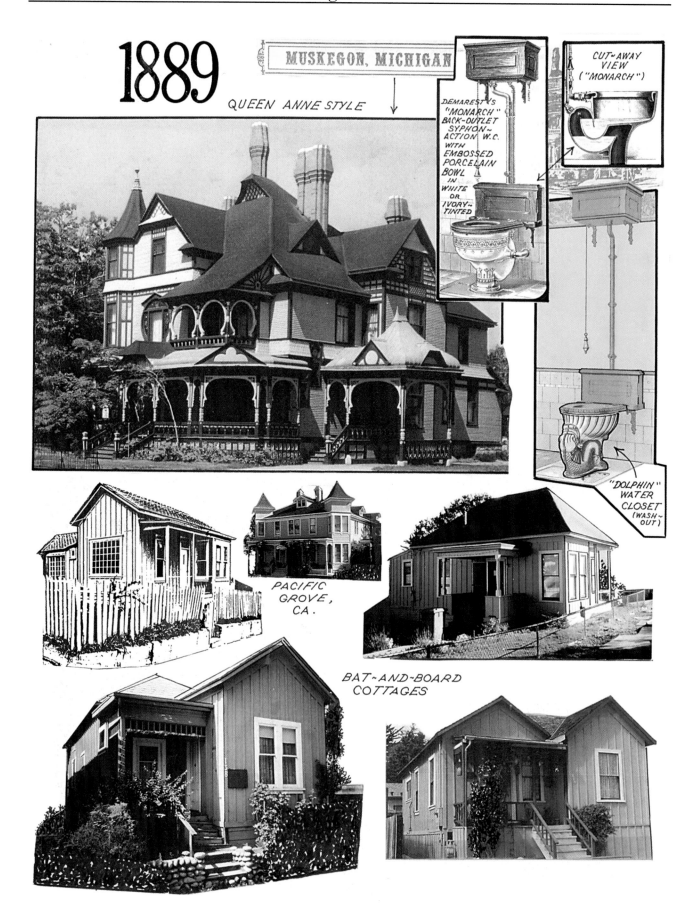

1889

MUSKEGON, MICHIGAN

QUEEN ANNE STYLE

DEMAREST'S "MONARCH" BACK-OUTLET SYPHON-ACTION W.C. WITH EMBOSSED PORCELAIN BOWL IN WHITE OR IVORY-TINTED

CUT-AWAY VIEW ("MONARCH")

"DOLPHIN" WATER CLOSET (WASH-OUT)

PACIFIC GROVE, CA.

BAT-AND-BOARD COTTAGES

GOVERNOR'S MANSION, RALEIGH, N.C.

EARLY USE OF TILE ON BATHROOM WALLS

LUXURY BATHROOMS

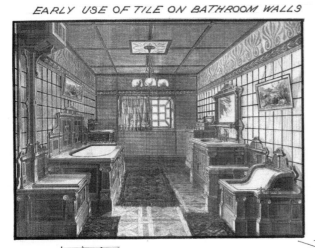

HAND~PAINTED TILES SET INTO FINE WOODEN CABINETWORK ENCLOSED AROUND FIXTURES

DIVIDED INTO 2 FLATS, AN 1889 HOUSE IN POOR CONDITION

SEMI~ENCLOSED HOPPER~TYPE WATER CLOSET (CUT~AWAY VIEW OF FRONT OF PLATFORM, TO SHOW FULL DETAIL)

1889

WELL~MAINTAINED

WITHOUT HISTORIC PRESERVATION, SOME VICTORIAN HOUSES BECAME RUN~DOWN SLUMS.

Chapter 2
1890-1899

The chief new style in this chapter is Neo-Classical Revival. These houses were inspired by ancient Roman temples, featuring columns (usually Tuscan—smooth and rounded), full pediments (triangles), Palladian windows (a large, round-headed center window flanked by rectangular smaller ones), and windows with "spider-web" tracery. Many were massive masonry piles, built to display the owner's wealth.

There are still "Victorian" houses. The Queen Anne, as one example, has asymmetrical roofs, towers, turrets, and bays, and yards of spindles, scrolls, and brackets. The Eastlake is contemporary with the Queen Anne, but has geometric ornament in place of the Queen Anne's circular scrolls and spindles. The Shingle Style came a few years later than Queen Anne. The main earmark of the Shingle Style was, not surprisingly, the shingles, which came in all shapes and sizes and covered the walls as well as the roofs.

Among the later styles introduced here is the so-called "Dutch Colonial," which featured a gambrel (barn) roof and Neoclassical Revival columns. It became a common style between about 1915 and 1930, but the later examples lost their classical details.

A final feature new to this chapter is the jerkin-head roof, in which a gable peak is flattened. This feature dates to at least as far back as medieval Europe, and it has reappeared here in what is referred to as a "New England Style."

The most significant cultural addition to this chapter is a very early car, the LeRoy, which dates to 1899. Many houses have now started to use electricity, and stamped steel ceilings have become popular.

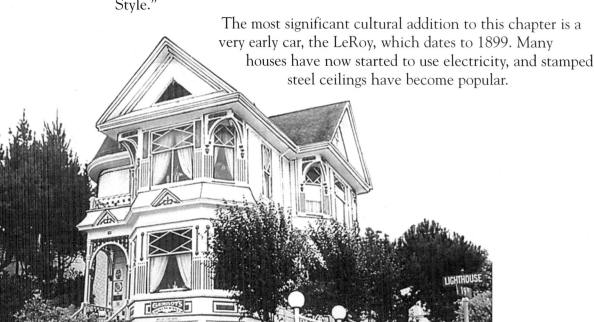

"MULBERRY PEACH" DECORATIVE W.C. BOWL (FOR USE WITH A HIGH TANK)
← OUTLET AT REAR

PACIFIC GROVE, CA.

LIMESTONE QUEEN ANNE MANSION MILWAUKEE, WI.

1890

ORIGINAL STYLE RETAINED, BUT THIS HOUSE SLIGHTLY EXPANDED.

INN →

FERNDALE, CA.

MOTT
PAINTED IRON
BATHTUB

2-FAMILY
HOUSE

← (OUTSIDE
STAIRWAY TO
UPPER UNIT)

1890

1890
SCHWARZWAELDER
DESK
← (ALL DIVISIONS
ARE
ADJUSTABLE)

FREE-STANDING FIXTURES GAINED
POPULARITY IN THE 1890s.

FRONT-
OUTLET
"WASHOUT"
TYPE

"ROMAN" W.C.

Victorian

DETAIL

WOODLAND, CA.
(WITH EASTLAKE and
QUEEN ANNE
ARCHITECTURAL DETAIL)

1890

EARLY
FIXTURES
LATER
REPLACED
BY NEW
UP-TO-DATE
TYPES,
AS IN
THIS
1927
AD.
←

WATER
CLOSET
("UNDINE"
WASHOUT
TYPE)

PULL~
CHAIN

WOOD

CISTERNS
(SUPPLY TANKS)

SUPPLY
PIPE

CUT~AWAY SIDE VIEW (BOWL)

WATER

VENT
PIPE

WALL

IRON

ABOVE : CUT~AWAY
VIEWS OF CISTERNS

WATER

PORCELAIN
"UNDINE" BOWL

SEWER

FLOOR

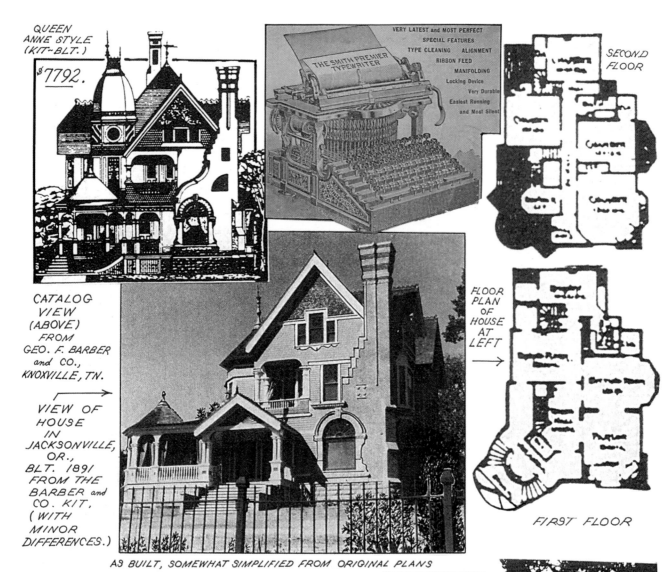

QUEEN
ANNE STYLE
(KIT-BLT.)

$7792.

VERY LATEST and MOST PERFECT
SPECIAL FEATURES
TYPE CLEANING   ALIGNMENT
RIBBON FEED
MANIFOLDING
Locking Device
Very Durable
Easiest Running
and Most Silent

THE SMITH PREMIER TYPEWRITER

SECOND FLOOR

CATALOG
VIEW
(ABOVE)
FROM
GEO. F. BARBER
and CO.,
KNOXVILLE, TN.

VIEW OF
HOUSE
IN
JACKSONVILLE,
OR.,
BLT. 1891
FROM THE
BARBER and
CO. KIT.
(WITH
MINOR
DIFFERENCES.)

FLOOR
PLAN
OF
HOUSE
AT
LEFT

FIRST FLOOR

AS BUILT, SOMEWHAT SIMPLIFIED FROM ORIGINAL PLANS

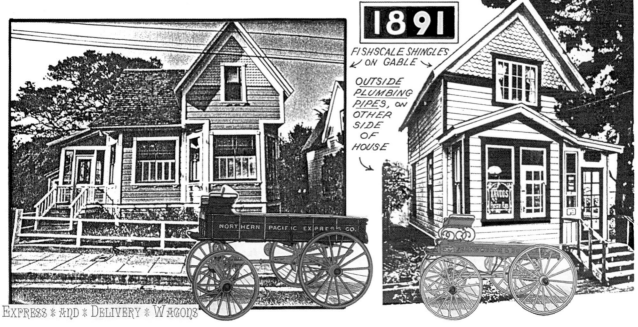

1891

FISHSCALE SHINGLES
ON GABLE

OUTSIDE
PLUMBING
PIPES, ON
OTHER
SIDE
OF
HOUSE

NORTHERN PACIFIC EXPRESS CO.

EXPRESS * AND * DELIVERY * WAGONS

WITH LARGE ATTIC

"It rests the back."

THE PERFECT CHAIR
For Piano, Sewing-Machine,
Desk and Typewriter.

BAY WINDOW

COMBINATION GABLED and HIP ROOF

OROVILLE, CA.

DERBY

VERTICAL BAT-and-BOARD SIDING, with TRUNCATED HIP ROOF PORT OVER DOOR with FLAT HOOD, BRACKETING

DIAGONAL BAY

HORIZONTAL SIDING

HIGH CEILINGS, AS SEEN BY TALL WINDOWS

5 MILLION WOMEN IN THE WORK FORCE BY 1891.

1891

TOP HAT

BEACH COTTAGE WITH BAY WINDOW

FISHSCALE SHINGLES IN GABLE, CLAPBOARD SIDING

HIP ROOF

CUT~AWAY CORNERS

STAIRWAYS WERE OFTEN INSTALLED BY A SPECIALIST

STAIR BUILDER.

ADS FROM A RARE 1891 SAN FRANCISCO CITY DIRECTORY, ONE OF VERY FEW WHICH SURVIVED THE 1906 EARTHQUAKE AND FIRE!

AN 1891 WELLS FARGO WAGON

A BELLE OF 1891

DECORATIVE FIGURE ON NEWELL POST

1676   SAN FRANCISCO DIRECTORY.

THE JOSEPH BUDDE'S POPULAR GOLDEN GATE.

With Trap.   With Offset.

Ocean Spray, Embossed Front and Cliff-Stream, Back Washout Closets,

WITH TANK AND MAHOGANY SEAT ATTACHED.

Are the best made and guaranted for 2 years. Gold Medal awarded at State Fair, 1888-89. Send for circular and price list.

Factory, N. W. cor. First and Mission Sts.

—ALSO—

Successor to WM. SMITH, 21 Montgomery Ave.

JOSEPH BUDDE;

And Manufacturer of the Improved Syphon Jet Closet.

ORIGINAL 1891 PLUMBING AD. (ABOVE)

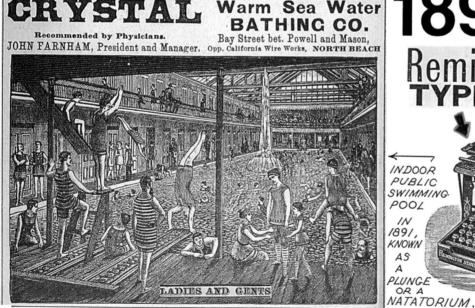

TERMINUS OF ALL NORTH BEACH CAR LINES.

CRYSTAL Warm Sea Water BATHING CO.

Recommended by Physicians.
JOHN FARNHAM, President and Manager.

Bay Street bet. Powell and Mason,
Opp. California Wire Works, **NORTH BEACH**

LADIES AND GENTS

1891

100,000

Remington Std. TYPEWRITERS

SINCE 1876

INDOOR PUBLIC SWIMMING POOL IN 1891, KNOWN AS A PLUNGE OR A NATATORIUM.

VICTORIAN garden

1892

BAT~and~BOARD
VERNACULAR
COTTAGE

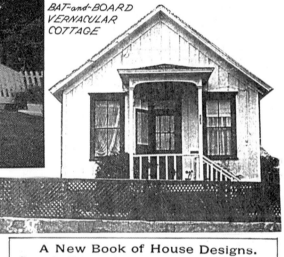

RESTORED, WITH
IMPROVEMENTS (ABOVE)

SAME HOUSE,
BEFORE →
RESTORATION

STANDARD

IN BUILDING A HOUSE

it is well to know that the difference
between the Standard Porcelain-lined
Bath Tubs and other kinds is
that the Standard baths
are absolutely pure inside,
and as beautiful as you
please without.

DECORATIVE
SQUARED~
CORNER
TUB

BY
STANDARD,
Pittsburgh

A New Book of House Designs.

Second edition pub-
lished
Feb. 15,
1892.
116 pp.

**Artistic
Dwellings**

A $2,000
Dwelling.

BY
FRANK P. ALLEN, Architect,
Grand Rapids, Mich.

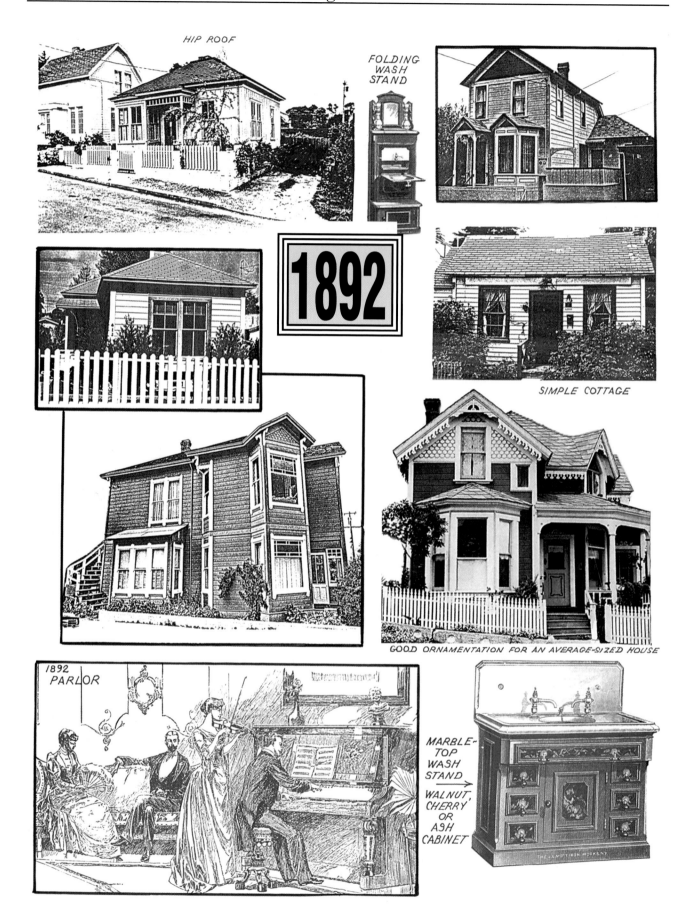

HIP ROOF

FOLDING WASH STAND

1892

SIMPLE COTTAGE

GOOD ORNAMENTATION FOR AN AVERAGE-SIZED HOUSE

1892 PARLOR

MARBLE-TOP WASH STAND

WALNUT, CHERRY OR ASH CABINET

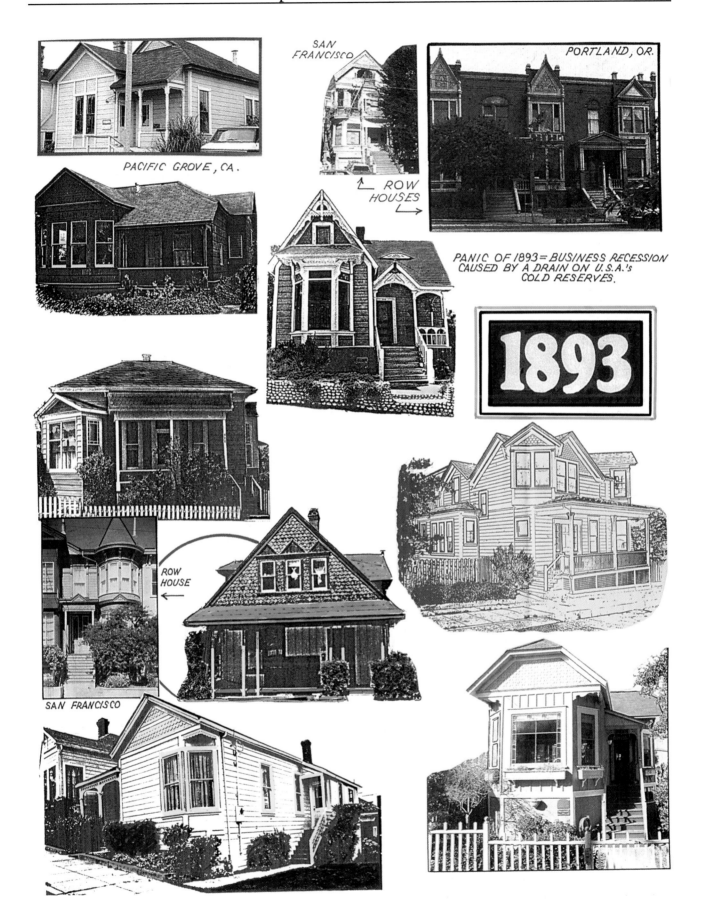

PACIFIC GROVE, CA.

SAN FRANCISCO

↑ ROW HOUSES →

PORTLAND, OR.

PANIC OF 1893 = BUSINESS RECESSION CAUSED BY A DRAIN ON U.S.A.'s COLD RESERVES.

1893

← ROW HOUSE

SAN FRANCISCO

NOBLESVILLE, INDIANA

QUEEN
ANNE
STYLE

OPEN GALLERY (ATRIUM), STAIRWAYS AND OPEN ELEVATOR SHAFT IN THE 1893 BRADBURY BLDG., IN LOS ANGELES (WHICH IS PRESERVED IN MUCH OF ITS ORIGINAL STATE!) →

GLASS ROOF ABOVE

1893

HOUSE IN PACIFIC GROVE, CALIF., AS IT ONCE APPEARED (ABOVE), AND AS IT LOOKS SINCE THE 1990s WHEN IT WAS AN ITALIAN RESTAURANT AND THE NEW EXTENSION ADDED

PASADENA, CA.
Queen Anne

WORK OF VICTORIAN ARCHITECTS

TYPICAL TURRET

WITH SQUARED BAY WINDOW

Carmel, CA.

DIAGONAL GABLE

PARTIAL HIP ROOF

2~FAMILY HOUSE IN PACIFIC GROVE, CA.

HEAVILY~DECORATED FREE-STANDING TUBS IN STYLE

(ABOVE) MOTT BATHTUB

EASTLAKE STYLE

1894

SAN FRANCISCO, CA.

LANSING, MI.

BAY WINDOW

NICELY RESTORED

PACIFIC GROVE, CA.

PACIFIC GROVE, CA.

PARLORS

HART MANSION

CURVED STAIRCASE

CLOSER DETAILS OF
UPPER FACADE,
WITH QUEEN ANNE
"GINGERBREAD"

1894

Wine and hors d'oeuvres are served in
the front parlor

← IN
RECENT YEARS,
THE MAIN FLOOR
HAS SERVED
AS A
FRENCH
Restaurant

MANY FARMS
ARE ABANDONED
WHEN SEVERE
DROUGHT HITS
THE MIDWEST.

ENTRY

2-STORY BAY WINDOW EXTENSION

1895

SEATTLE, WA.

BRIDGEPORT, CT.

SYMMETRICAL STYLE

NOT ALL HOMES HAD ELECTRICITY IN 1895

1895 OIL LAMP

SANTA CRUZ, CA.

OLD VIEW (UNRESTORED) (RESTORED VIEW, LOWER RT.)

SMALL "QUEEN ANNE" STYLE HOUSE

1895 HOUSES IN PACIFIC GROVE, CA.

BAT-AND-BOARD COTTAGE

RECENT VIEW (RESTORED)

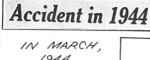

Accident in 1944

IN MARCH, 1944, 3 MEN WERE KILLED WHEN THEIR NAVY TORPEDO BOMBER CRASHED ON THE GROUNDS OF THIS RESIDENCE, NARROWLY MISSING THE MANSION, ITSELF! CAUSE OF THE CRASH: POWER LINES WHICH SNAGGED THE LOW~FLYING AIRCRAFT.

LA PORTE MANSION
PACIFIC GROVE, CA.

THIS LOVELY 1895 VICTORIAN WAS FILMED IN 1959 FOR MUCH OF THE BACKGROUND FOR "A SUMMER PLACE."

(THE SETTING FOR THE MOVIE'S FICTITIOUS STORY WAS THE EAST COAST, HOWEVER!)

QUEEN ANNE STYLE

1895

GAZEBO ON THE GROUNDS OF THE LA PORTE MANSION

← CLOSER DETAILS

AMERICA'S LARGEST HOME

NEAR ASHEVILLE, N.C.

OPEN TO THE PUBLIC SINCE 1930

FRENCH CHATEAU STYLE

the grandest of all the American palaces.

NO LID OVER SEAT

LOW~DOWN~TANK TOILET (MORE MODERN STYLE THAN THE PAIR SEEN AT LOWER LEFT.)

250~ROOM MANSION, "BILTMORE HOUSE" BLT. FOR G.W. VANDERBILT, NEAR ASHEVILLE, N.C.

2 VANDERBILT MANSIONS

Bath Cabinet.
A CURE for Rheumatism, Liver and Skin Diseases, Etc.

STEAM BATH

CLASSIC REVIVAL STYLE

1895

"THE BREAKERS", 70~ROOM MANSION BLT. FOR CORNELIUS VANDERBILT AT NEWPORT, L.I., N.Y. (FIREPROOF 1895 REPLACEMENT FOR EARLIER MANSION BURNED 1892)

"RAISED ACANTHUS"

DECORATIVE WATER CLOSET BOWLS (WASHOUT TYPE)

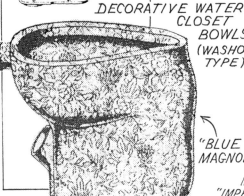

"BLUE MAGNOLIA"

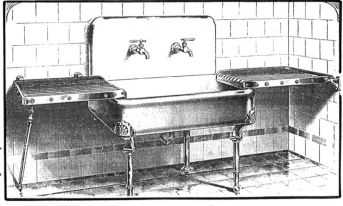

MOTT "IMPERIAL" ROLL~RIM KITCHEN SINK (PORCELAIN, with ASH~WOOD DRAIN~BOARDS)

SEAVIEW, WA.

FULLY~
SHINGLED
EXTERIOR
WALLS A
RELATIVELY
NEW IDEA
IN
LATE 1890s.

HIP ROOF

BAT~
AND~
BOARD
COTTAGE

PACIFIC GROVE, CA.

1896

SALINAS, CA.

"STEAMBOAT COLONIAL"
GAMBREL ROOF, DORMERS,
SEMI-CIRCULAR PORCH and BALCONY
(SOME IMPROVEMENTS IN 1910)

TUB ON WHEELS!

STEEL CLAD BATH CO. of N.Y.

SIDE~FILLING BATHTUB

Copyright by THE J. L. MOTT IRON WORKS.   Design No. 12.   Reduced cut.   Plate 1306 G.

IMPERIAL PORCELAIN ROLL-RIM BATHS.

Fine appearance, durability, and perfection from a sanitary standpoint are all combined in these goods. They entail no labor, scouring or burnishing, requiring merely to be wiped out with a sponge to be thoroughly cleaned.
  Imperial Porcelain Ware, with its substantial thickness, fine glaze, and beautiful appearance, is the ideal material for Sanitary appliances. Our revised prices bring the cost of Porcelain goods to a figure at which they can be advantageously used in all fine and moderate-priced dwellings; also in hospitals, etc.

SAN DIEGO, CA.

OLD~FASHIONED "FISH~SCALE" DECORATIVE SHINGLES STILL POPULAR TO ENHANCE UPPER GABLES IN 1897.

1897

THIS UNUSUALLY BROAD, PYRAMID~ROOFED COTTAGE OF 1897 WAS PRACTICE~ BURNED BY THE FIRE DEPT. IN 1986, TO CLEAR THE LAND FOR 2 NEW HOUSES.

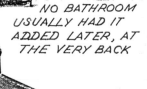

PACIFIC GROVE, CA.

HOUSES THAT ORIGINALLY HAD NO BATHROOM USUALLY HAD IT ADDED LATER, AT THE VERY BACK

THIS "QUEEN ANNE" VICTORIAN HOUSE IS THE BIRTHPLACE AND FAMOUS AUTHOR

STEINBECK

SALINAS, CA. CHILDHOOD HOME OF JOHN STEINBECK. NOW OPEN TO THE PUBLIC.

HOUSE

LOVINGTON, IL.

AN AMERICAN FLAG HAS BEEN PAINTED ON THE WALL SINCE THIS HOUSE WAS NEW IN 1897!

SALINAS, CA.

QUEEN ANNE VICTORIAN

TUTTLE MANSION

WATSONVILLE, CA.

(COMPLETED 1899)

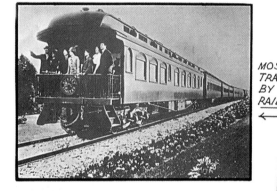

MOST INTERCITY
TRAVEL WAS
BY
RAIL.
←

new 2-STORY ECLECTIC
"BOX" STYLE

SHINGLED
WALLS

1898

NEW ENGLAND
STYLE

HIP
ROOF

BOX
SHAPE
WITH
FLAT
ROOF
OVER
FRONT
PORCH

EARLY APT. HOUSE

PACIFIC GROVE, CA.

37~ROOM DUNSMUIR MANSION OAKLAND, CA. 11 BEDROOMS, 7 BATHS COST $250,000. TO BUILD IN 1898 !!

↖ CLASSIC REVIVAL STYLE

New York.

1898

ARCHITECTURE;

QUEEN ANNE

SANTA CRUZ COUNTY, CA.

BAT~AND BOARD, WITH BAY~FRONT GABLE, RANCH~STYLE PORCH ←

← HIGH TANK UNUSUALLY LOCATED AT ONE SIDE OF W.C. INSTEAD OF AT THE REAR.

COTTAGE

SHINGLED UPPER STORY

MORE MODERN
STYLES BEGIN
TO MAKE THEIR
APPEARANCE.

1899

DECORATIVE ALCOVE

HIP
ROOF
WITH
DIAGONAL
GABLE

A
RESTORED
1899
INTERIOR

FARMHOUSE
STYLE

NOTICE
THE
HALF~
DORMERS.

PACIFIC GROVE, CA.

CALIFORNIA
STYLES

BEACH COTTAGE WITH
ENCLOSED
PORCH

RANCH STYLE FRONT PORCH

NEW

← DUTCH →
COLONIAL
STYLE

(TWO EARLY EXAMPLES
OF 1899. THIS
STYLE MORE POPULAR
TWO DECADES LATER!)

DENVER, CO.

GAMBREL ROOF AND DORMERS ARE
TYPICAL OF DUTCH COLONIALS.

1899

HEAVILY-EMBOSSED,
DECORATIVE, FIREPROOF

STEEL CEILINGS

MANY
DESIGNS

FROM H.S. NORTHROP (CO.), NYC

1899 LE ROY
HORSELESS
CARRIAGE

Planetary Pencil Pointer

Needed
in
every
Home
and
School.

Not a Toy,
But a
Machine.

Circular
Free.

Never breaks the point. Preserves the softest
lead. Saves its cost in the saving of lead. Cleanly,
convenient, useful.

Made only by A. B. DICK COMPANY,
152-154 Lake Street, CHICAGO.

SAVANNAH,
GA.
←

"STEAMBOAT
GOTHIC" STYLE
ORNATE
2 STORY
PORCH

SHINGLED
HIP~ROOFED
COTTAGE
UP~TO
DATE,
WITH NO
"GINGERBREAD"
ORNAMENTATION.

← MOST PEOPLE TODAY HAVE NEVER SEEN
PLUMBING FIXTURES OF THE
19TH CENTURY.

Chapter 3

1900-1909

A few of the styles introduced in this chapter have come to dominate the first half of the twentieth century, so in a sense, this was the first modern decade.

One, the Craftsman/Bungalow, was the most prevalent style in the 1910s. The second, the Prairie style, did not show up in many whole houses, but was influential in general. Designed and built by many architects, it was best known as Frank Lloyd Wright's ideal of the natural house—long, low, and using earth materials and colors.

Another influential style was the American Foursquare, a two-and-a-half-story cube with a hip or deck roof, an "attic dormer," and a wide front porch supported by Tuscan columns or Craftsman battered (tapered from bottom to top) posts. It came to dominate city residential streets, and was, in some ways, an echo of the Italianate styles, which were square or rectangular houses with hip or deck roofs, wide (often bracketed) eaves, and segmental-arched (slightly round-headed) windows.

Last were the Colonial Revival styles. These included the New England Colonial with its saltbox roofs and/or asymmetrical gables, and garrison (second-story) overhangs. The Federal, which usually had gabled roofs, and the Georgian, with its hip or deck roofs, are other examples. All of these were large two story or two and a half story houses with symmetrical doors and small-pane windows, dormers, and classical details.

An important innovation at this time was the mail-order house from Sears, Roebuck & Company and its competitors. Offering modestly sized and priced houses, these companies spread the era's dominant styles around the nation, allowing many families to have new houses, and later helping to solve the post-World War I housing shortage. Also called kit-houses, they were ordered complete—lumber, nails, lath, plaster, doors, windows, millwork (frames/casings), hinges, locks, flooring, roofing shingles, paint, and varnish. All these materials were shipped in sealed boxcars. The owner provided only the lot, basement, and foundation.

Other new items included cement blocks, which gradually replaced stones for foundations and even upper walls; enclosed porches; steam radiators; basement furnaces with built-in water heaters; oak toilet-seats; sheetrock on interior walls; and outdoor faucets.

GABLED, DORMERED ROOF

1½~STORY

SHINGLED EXTERIORS and HIP ROOFS GROW IN POPULARITY

1~STORY

2-STORY

SHIP MODELS POPULAR

Babcock Carriage

1900 Waverley Electromobile "PIANO BOX" RUNABOUT

MODEL 18

193,000 MILES OF RAILROADS IN THE U.S.A. IN 1901.

ELECTRIC

1900

MOST URBAN and SUBURBAN HOMES WIRED FOR ELECTRICITY

AMERICAN-English STYLE (TUDOR)

BAT~and~BOARD WALLS

1~STORY

2-STORY

FEW FRONT PORCHES ENCLOSED AT TURN OF CENTURY. 1900

1901

OUTSIDE PLUMBING PIPES COMMON

VARIATIONS ON THIS NEW STYLE POPULAR FOR THE FOLLOWING 20 YEARS!

POPULAR BOOKS OF 1901, TYPICAL OF THOSE FOUND IN MANY HOMES!

THE FALL OF THE CURTAIN
A Brilliant Society Novel

FLOATING TREASURE
BY HARRY CASTLEMON

COWARDICE·COURT
GEORGE·BARR·M°CUTCHEON

Lives of the Hunted
Ernest Seton-Thompson

SHOW
AUTOMOBILE CLUB
of AMERICA
Madison Square Garden
NOVEMBER 3RD TO 10TH 1900.

MALCOLM A. STRAUSS

FANCY·DRESS·PARTY of 1901

2 EXAMPLES OF A FREQUENTLY·SEEN 1901 HOUSE ← STYLE → 2~WINDOW FRONT GABLE WITH ADJOINING PORCH

SMALL COTTAGE

FRONT ENTRY DETAILS →

PACIFIC GROVE, CA.

FRONT VIEW

3 VIEWS OF THIS INTERESTING HOUSE

FRONT / SIDE VIEW

1901 OFFICIAL END OF THE VICTORIAN ERA:

VICTORIA, ENGLAND'S QUEEN SINCE 1837, DIES IN 1901 AND IS SUCCEEDED BY HER SON, EDWARD VII, USHERING IN THE "EDWARDIAN" ERA

UP~TO~DATE BATHROOM OF 1901 (STANDARD PLUMBING FIXTURES)

FIRST MURPHY~BUILT HOUSE OF 1902
CARMEL, CA.

Acme Folding Bath Tubs with Instantaneous Heater Combined.

CLASSIC~STYLE MANSION

02

COTTAGE IN SEATTLE (PARTIALLY~SHINGLED EXTER.)

BAT~AND~BOARD COTTAGE

QUEEN ANNE STYLE "TWIN SISTERS", ALAMEDA, CALIF.

ACME HOT WATER HEATER

ACME STEAM OR HOT WATER RADIATOR, FOR HOME HEATING

1902 "CURVED DASH" OLDSMOBILE

"SHADELANDS" (WALNUT CREEK, CALIF.)

IN SACRAMENTO, CALIF. →

(SIMILAR TO OTHERS SEEN IN ALL PARTS OF U.S.A.)

02

(MUCH STONEWORK ON THE GROUND FLOOR IS OPTIONAL.)

ECLECTIC STYLE with BOW, BAY and DORMER WINDOWS (ABOVE) (A MODERN DEPARTURE FROM THE PREVIOUS VICTORIAN STYLES!)

DAYTON, OH.

EVER~READY FLASHLIGHT

(A.K.A. "ELECTRIC TORCH")

BEACON HOUSE PACIFIC GROVE, CALIF.

QUEEN ANNE STYLES

NOTE UNUSUAL OPENING IN THE FOYER CEILING, SO THAT THOSE UPSTAIRS COULD SEE THOSE WHO HAD ENTERED THE HOUSE.

Kearns *Mansion has 28 rooms, 6 baths, and 9 fireplaces. House was built in 1902 for Senator Thomas Kearns. It later was a governor's mansion. Above, visitors stand in main hallway below ornate ceiling well*

KEARNS MANSION (SALT LAKE CITY)

DUMB WAITER

GOTHIC TUDOR REVIVAL MANSION

1½-STORY WITH PARTIAL DORMER ABOVE FULL-WIDTH FRONT PORCH

Two Compartment Granitine Laundry Tubs. With High Back and Soap Cup.

1903

FLOOR PLAN OF HOUSE AT LOWER RIGHT (CENTRAL PATIO)

Kitchen

Dining

Living

Maid

BR

BR

BR

Patio

0   10   25'

NATURAL OAK TOILET SEAT AND LID CONTINUES IN POPULARITY.

TOWEL RACKS

IN PASADENA, CA.

RIVER-ROCK CHIMNEY

THE FIRST CALIFORNIA-RANCH STYLE HOME (1903) DESIGNED BY GREENE and GREENE, ARCHITECTS. BUILT AROUND A CENTRAL PATIO. MORE THAN 30 YEARS AHEAD OF ITS TIME!!

PATIO

FAUCETS

FOR TUB

1903

1903 FORD

BEACH COTTAGE ↑
(SHINGLED EXTERIOR)
(ABOVE)

OUTDOOR FAUCET

HARTFORD SINGLE TUBE
DUNLOP DOUBLE TUBE and
HARTFORD SOLID RUBBER
TIRES. Each the Best and
Most Durable of its Class

PORTABLE SHOWER YOKE and HOSE $1.20, FROM SEARS, ROEBUCK

THIS 1903 TIRE ADVERTISEMENT FORESHADOWED THE REPLACEMENT OF THE HORSE, BY THE HORSELESS CARRIAGE.

OLD~FASHIONED "GINGERBREAD" TRIM AT TOP OF GABLE and ABOVE PORCH

a good example of **Frank Lloyd Wright** ARCHITECTURE

ADVANCE DESIGN!

THIS HOUSE was built by Frank Lloyd Wright in 1904 for Buffalo businessman Darrow D. Martin, secretary of the Larkin Company.

BUFFALO, N.Y.

HOUSES WITH FULL~WIDTH COVERED PORCHES

NOTE THE EXTREME DIFFERENCES BETWEEN THESE 2 STYLES!

UP~TO~ DATE SHINGLE COTTAGE WITH HIP ROOF

PACIFIC GROVE, CA.

SELMA, CA.

QUEEN ANNE STYLE A BIT OUTDATED BY 1904.

1904

Latest Design
Bath Room

A DIFFERENT~ ANGLE, LATER VIEW OF HOUSE SHOWN DIRECTLY ABOVE

FRONT / SIDE VIEW

FRONT VIEW

LOW~ TANK TOILET, CLAW~ FOOT TUB, WALL-HUNG WASH BASIN and TILED FLOOR and WALLS

IF 2ND STORY IS WITHIN A GABLE, without VERTICAL EXTERIOR WALLS ON ALL SIDES, THAT HOUSE IS CONSIDERED TO BE "1½~STORY."

Rival Water Heater is a convenient and almost indespensable auxilary to a hot air furnace.

This cut shows Heater attached to hot air furnace.

9 BDRMS   3 BA

EARLY GARAGES ALSO KNOWN AS "AUTOMOBILE HOUSES."

BAY WINDOW

FULL~WIDTH PORCH

04

CLASSIC REVIVAL STYLE

IN BERKELEY, CA.

FISHSCALE SHINGLES ON UPPER GABLE, (ATTIC), BAT~AND~BOARD ON MAIN LEVEL

M & M PORTABLE HOUSES

ONE WAY

BAT~AND~BOARD COTTAGE

VERNACULAR~
STYLE
RENTAL
COTTAGE

BERKELEY, CA.

Gramma's

Breakfast Inn

APRIL, 1905

SINK

Full blue print
working plans
and specifica-
tions complete.
No. 52

PREMIER PORTABLE Pleasure=Houses
$35 - $60

05

Wᴹ READ & SONS.
TRADE MARK
·BOSTON, MASS·

THESE
19ᵀᴴ-CENTURY-STYLE
"ELEPHANT" WASHOUT
WATER CLOSETS STILL
BEING INSTALLED
IN SOME
HOMES
OF 1905.

THIS PLAN CAN BE REVERSED TO SUIT LOCATION

THIS superb **Colonial dwelling** with its modern reception hall, opening into a large parlor with pretty fireplace, good size dining room with artistic bay window effect, up-to-date kitchen arrangement, large pantry and cupboards. **Three good sized chambers on second floor,** with bath-room conveniently arranged and accessible from all rooms. Large front porch, 7-foot stoned-up basement, first story 9 feet, second story 8½ feet. Dining room, parlor and hall finished in hard wood, kitchen and bedrooms in Georgia pine.

CUPBOARD
PANTRY
8'6" × 5'

KITCHEN
12' × 10'

Down

DINING
12' × 14'

Clo:

Seat

RECEP.
HALL
12' × 13'

Grille
Grille

PARLOR
13' × 15'

PIAZZA
10' × 11'

Isn't
this a
Beauty?

170 more
homes like
this for 25c.
Built Over
300 Times
For $1150
Complete
Including
Plumbing

**OUR
BIG
BOOK**

of 170
homes for
25 cents
(silver)

Regular
price $1.00

Send 9c. for
postage if
you please

clo
Alcove

BED ROOM
14' × 10'

Closet

Bed Rm
13' × 12'

Hall
Down

BATH
6' × 8'6"

Closet

Bed Rm
14' × 12'

SECOND FLOOR

J. H. DAVERMAN & SON, Arch'ts, 404 Porter Block, Grand Rapids, Mich. Estab. 1882

← ATTIC DORMERS →
STYLISH IN
1906

EDWARDIAN ECLECTIC STYLE

BAY TURRET

RARE!
ADVERTISED
ALSO IN
1905,
BUT NOT
GENERALLY
ACCEPTED.

NATURO

The Closet with a slant. The only closet in harmony with the natural laws of Physiology and Hygiene. Free Book 48 explains fully. Send for it.
The Naturo Company - Salem, N. J., U. S. A.

STAIRWAY

TERRE
HAUTE,
IN.
←

WHEN YOU BUILD
use
Concrete Blocks
←

A GRADUALLY
INCREASING
USE OF
THIN
SHIPLAP
CLAPBOARD
SIDING,
UNTIL
EARLY
1930s.

DUTCH COLONIAL

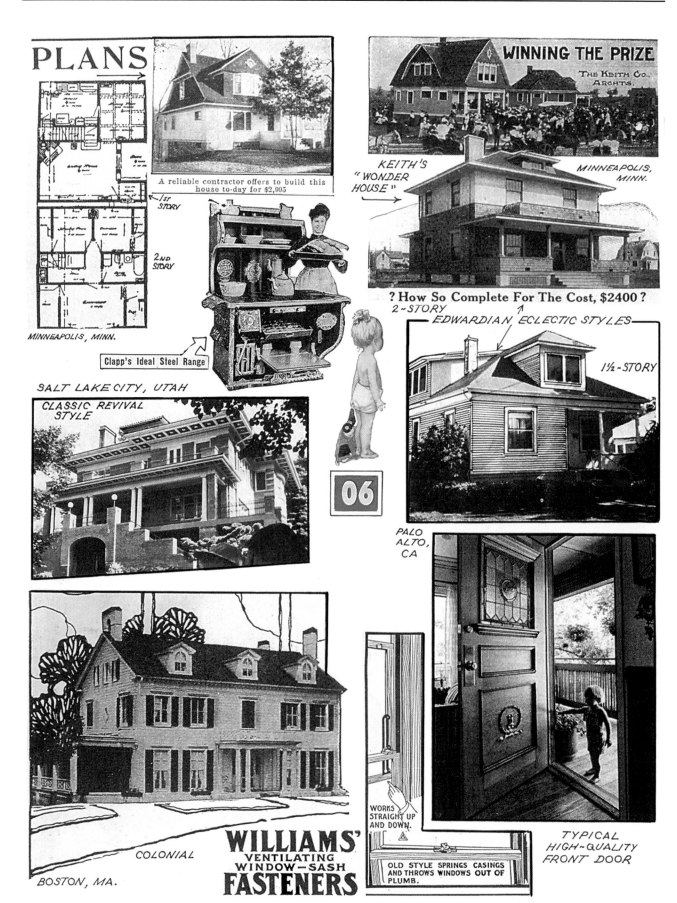

PLANS

A reliable contractor offers to build this house to-day for $2,995

1st STORY

2nd STORY

MINNEAPOLIS, MINN.

Clapp's Ideal Steel Range

SALT LAKE CITY, UTAH

CLASSIC REVIVAL STYLE

WINNING THE PRIZE

THE KEITH CO. ARCHTS.

KEITH'S "WONDER HOUSE"

MINNEAPOLIS, MINN.

? How So Complete For The Cost, $2400 ?

2-STORY

EDWARDIAN ECLECTIC STYLES

1½-STORY

06

PALO ALTO, CA

COLONIAL

BOSTON, MA.

WILLIAMS' VENTILATING WINDOW—SASH **FASTENERS**

WORKS STRAIGHT UP AND DOWN.

OLD STYLE SPRINGS CASINGS AND THROWS WINDOWS OUT OF PLUMB.

TYPICAL HIGH-QUALITY FRONT DOOR

THIS DESIGN "OLD-HAT" STYLE BY 1907.

MacLagan Suburban Homes

NEWARK, N.J.

Elkhart Carriage & Harness Mfg. Co., Elkhart, Ind.

CLOSET

BATH ROOM

PANTRY

Plan

MINNEAPOLIS, MINN.

1907

1907 KLINK

EARLY-DAY SHEETROCK AVAILABLE IN 32" x 36" SECTIONS, FROM:

UNITED STATES GYPSUM CO.
CHICAGO   CLEVELAND   FT. DODGE

GRAND RAPIDS PLASTER CO.
GRAND RAPIDS, MICH.

SACKETT PLASTER BOARD COMPANY, 17 BATTERY PL., N. Y. CITY

BURLINGAME

SYMMETRICAL BAT-AND-BOARD COTTAGE

DOORS

1908

HIGH GRADE ROLL RIM WHITE PORCELAIN ENAMELED BATH TUB $18.85

LEADED~GLASS WINDOW

MODIFIED QUEEN ANNE STYLE

HALF MOON BAY, CA.

MARBLE LAV- $9.05

CHALET STYLE

1908 CORBIN

SHINGLED WALLS POPULAR

5~ CROSS- PANEL INSIDE DOOR

ARCHED ENTRIES

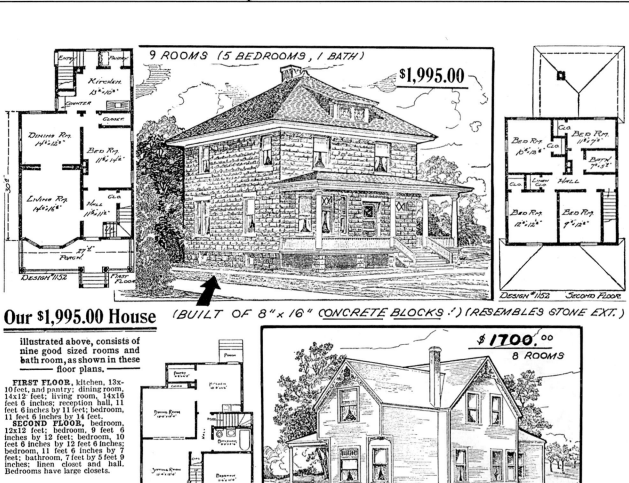

9 ROOMS (5 BEDROOMS, 1 BATH)

$1,995.00

DESIGN #1152 FIRST FLOOR

DESIGN #1152 SECOND FLOOR

Our $1,995.00 House

(BUILT OF 8" x 16" CONCRETE BLOCKS!) (RESEMBLES STONE EXT.)

illustrated above, consists of nine good sized rooms and bath room, as shown in these floor plans.

FIRST FLOOR, kitchen, 13x-10 feet, and pantry; dining room, 14x12 feet; living room, 14x16 feet 6 inches; reception hall, 11 feet 6 inches by 11 feet; bedroom, 11 feet 6 inches by 14 feet.

SECOND FLOOR, bedroom, 12x12 feet; bedroom, 9 feet 6 inches by 12 feet; bedroom, 10 feet 6 inches by 12 feet 6 inches; bedroom, 11 feet 6 inches by 7 feet; bathroom, 7 feet by 5 feet 9 inches; linen closet and hall. Bedrooms have large closets.

08

$1700.00
8 ROOMS

FIRST FLOOR PLAN.

FRAME (CLAPBOARD) EXTERIOR

KITS FOR BUILDING THESE HOUSES WERE AVAILABLE FROM SEARS, ROEBUCK IN 1908, FOR THE FIRST TIME

PLAN

SECOND FLOOR PLAN.

6~ROOM COUNTRY FARMHOUSE (NO BATHROOM)

OUR $725.00 HOUSE, ILLUSTRATED

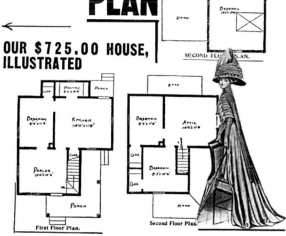

First Floor Plan.

Second Floor Plan.

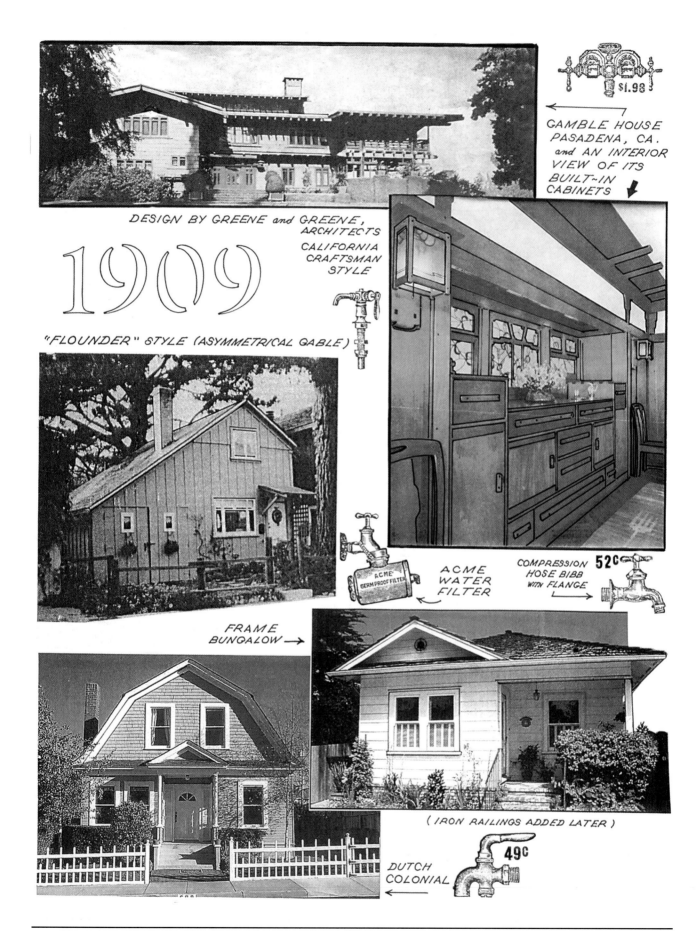

$1.98

GAMBLE HOUSE
PASADENA, CA.
and AN INTERIOR
VIEW OF ITS
BUILT~IN
CABINETS

DESIGN BY GREENE and GREENE,
ARCHITECTS

CALIFORNIA
CRAFTSMAN
STYLE

1909

"FLOUNDER" STYLE (ASYMMETRICAL GABLE)

ACME
WATER
FILTER

ACME
GERM PROOF FILTER

COMPRESSION
HOSE BIBB
WITH FLANGE

52¢

FRAME
BUNGALOW →

(IRON RAILINGS ADDED LATER)

DUTCH
COLONIAL →

49¢

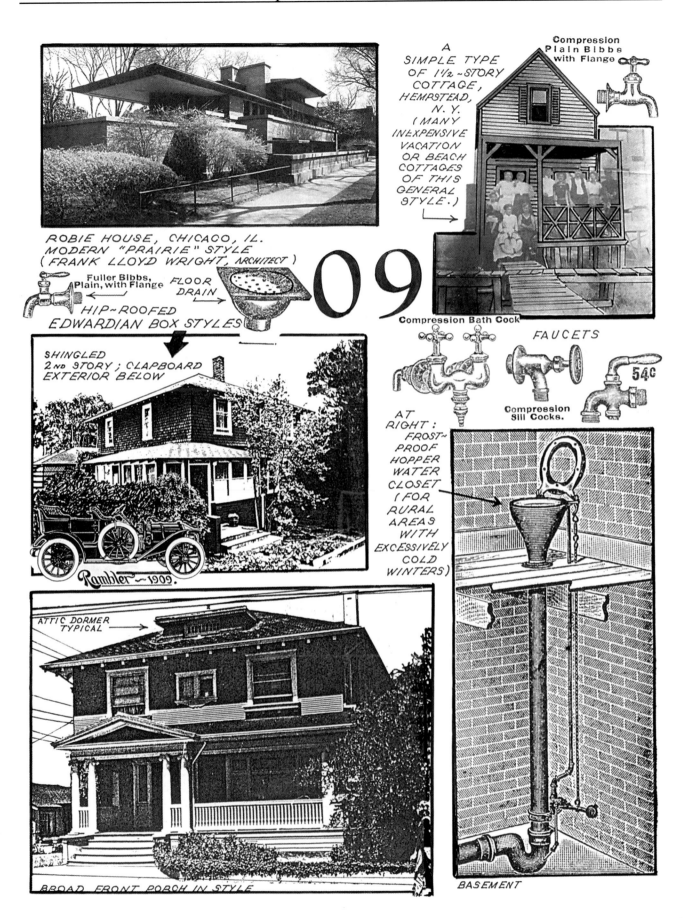

ROBIE HOUSE, CHICAGO, IL.
MODERN "PRAIRIE" STYLE
(FRANK LLOYD WRIGHT, ARCHITECT)

A SIMPLE TYPE OF 1½~STORY COTTAGE, HEMPSTEAD, N.Y. (MANY INEXPENSIVE VACATION OR BEACH COTTAGES OF THIS GENERAL STYLE.)

Compression Plain Bibbs with Flange

Fuller Bibbs, Plain, with Flange

FLOOR DRAIN

HIP~ROOFED EDWARDIAN BOX STYLES

'09

Compression Bath Cock

FAUCETS

Compression Sill Cocks.

54¢

SHINGLED 2ND STORY; CLAPBOARD EXTERIOR BELOW

Rambler ~ 1909.

AT RIGHT: FROST~ PROOF HOPPER WATER CLOSET (FOR RURAL AREAS WITH EXCESSIVELY COLD WINTERS)

ATTIC DORMER TYPICAL

BROAD FRONT PORCH IN STYLE

BASEMENT

Chapter 4

1910-1919

This period was the heyday of the Craftsman/Bungalow styles. They came in many variations on two basic models. The Bungalow (Western Stick Style) was a long, narrow, one-story, gabled house with a single ridgepole, a front door in the end, and was modeled after ranch bunkhouses. The Bungaloid had wide gables, a front door in the side, and a large dormer over the integrated (by a common roof) front porch. But most Bungaloids and Bungalows had exposed rafter ends, strut brackets, shed (slanted, single-plane) roofs, and battered posts. On the interior, there were exposed ceiling-beams, paneling, and fireplaces with "inglenooks" (little recesses), all in dark-oak woodwork in simple square (Mission) designs.

Related to the Craftsman/Bungalow styles was the "rustic" trend, a movement that took city dwellers back to the land. This included rustic-looking houses, some now built of redwood lumber, with "fresh-air sleeping porches" or sunrooms.

On the other hand, high technology and modern materials took the nation further into the new century. "Metal lumber"—steel beams and studs—debuted during this decade, but was rarely used.

Stucco, an exterior plaster that originated in the ancient world, was revived for use on many houses between 1910 and 1940. It often looked like stone, it could have various designs molded or brushed into it, and at its best it was very hard and durable. It gained popularity during the 1920s.

Finally, many inventions changed our lives inside houses during this decade. Candlestick telephones became popular, as did electric appliances like toasters, vacuum cleaners, coffee pots, irons, and kitchen ranges. Hoosier prefabricated kitchen cabinets, thermostats, and "noiseless" toilets were also becoming a part of the average house.

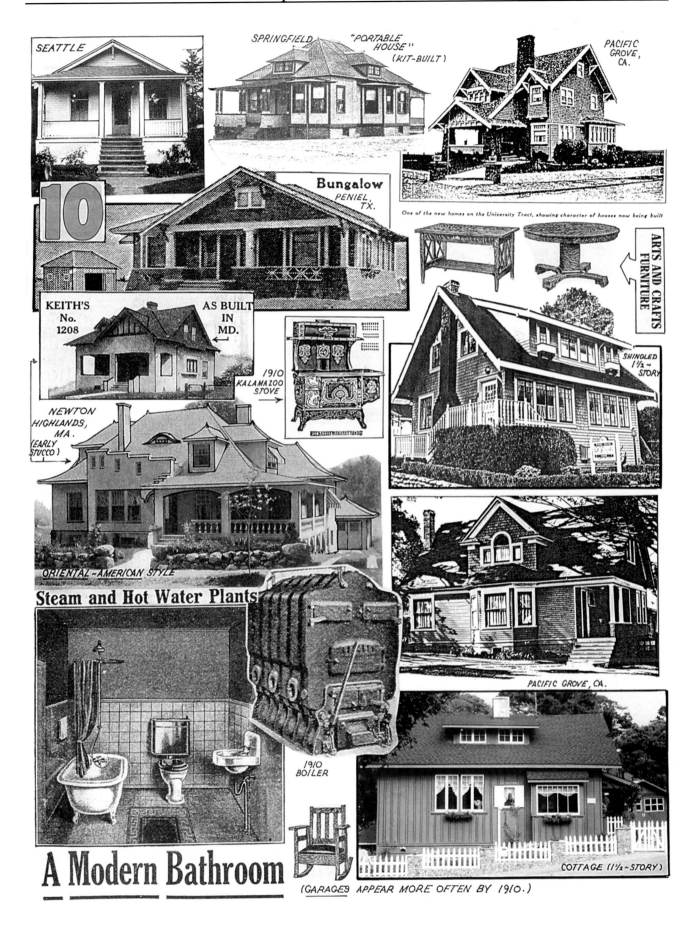

SEATTLE

SPRINGFIELD "PORTABLE HOUSE" (KIT-BUILT)

PACIFIC GROVE, CA.

One of the new homes on the University Tract, showing character of houses now being built

10

Bungalow PENIEL, TX.

ARTS AND CRAFTS FURNITURE

KEITH'S No. 1208

AS BUILT IN MD. ←

1910 KALAMAZOO STOVE →

SHINGLED 1½ STORY

NEWTON HIGHLANDS, MA. (EARLY STUCCO)

ORIENTAL ~ AMERICAN STYLE

Steam and Hot Water Plants

PACIFIC GROVE, CA.

1910 BOILER

A Modern Bathroom

COTTAGE (1½ ~ STORY)

(GARAGES APPEAR MORE OFTEN BY 1910.)

UKIAH, CA.

11

N.Y.

THIS $419. KIT HOUSE had 4 ROOMS BUT **NO** BATHROOM!

HASTINGS, NE.

SEARS ROEBUCK KIT HOUSE and FLOOR PLAN
DULUTH, MN.

DINING ROOM

FRENCH DOORS

MAHOGANY or OAK WOODWORK POPULAR

LIVING ROOM

BAY WINDOW

D.R.
PANTRY
K.
L.R.
FRONT PORCH
PORCH
DOWNSTAIRS

UPSTAIRS
PORCH ROOF
B.R.
BATH
B.R.
HALL
CLOSET CLOSET
B.R.
B.R.

living room

SAN RAFAEL, CA.

2~STORY
FRONT
BAY
WINDOWS

2~FAMILY FLAT
OLNEYVILLE, R.I.

SEARS, ROEBUCK
KIT HOUSES

HUNTINGTON,
W. VA.

"Standard" GUARANTEED PLUMBING FIXTURES

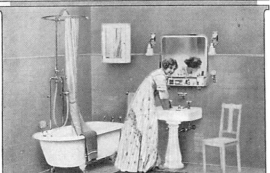

ABOVE:
2 ADS FOR "STANDARD" FIXTURES, DATED FEB., 1911 (TOP) and MAY, 1911 (BOTTOM) note SLIGHT DIFFERENCES IN TUB CLAWFEET and LAVATORY SINK, PEDESTAL TYPE.)

11

BIRCH INSIDE DOOR (2' 8" x 7')

WINDOW 2' x 4½'

THESE ITEMS (7) AVAIL. FROM SEARS, ROEBUCK

3' x 7' CRAFTSMAN OAK FRONT DOOR

CRAFTSMAN OAK INSIDE DOOR (2' 8" x 7')

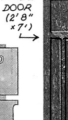

KITCHEN DOOR (PINE) (2' 8" x 7')

REAR OUTSIDE DOOR (3' x 7')

CORNELL GARAGES SECTIONAL PORTABLE

A Modern Bath
ALLEN MFG. CO.

BUFFET

"CHICAGO STYLE"

ANN ARBOR, MI.

✱ = SEARS, ROEBUCK
KIT HOUSE

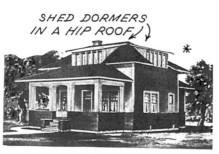

SHED DORMERS
IN A HIP ROOF ✱

STUCCO ON 1ST FLOOR   ✱   SIDE ENTRANCE

JOLIET, IL.

"CALIFORNIA ~ TYPE" BUNGALOW   SPRINGFIELD, MA.

B.R.   K

L.R.

B.R.   PORCH

DOWNSTAIRS FLOOR PLAN →

FLOOR
PLAN

12

Walnut Panelled Library

ROCK ISLAND, IL.

MEDITERRANEAN
STYLE

"MONTALVO"   LOS GATOS ~ SARATOGA, CA.

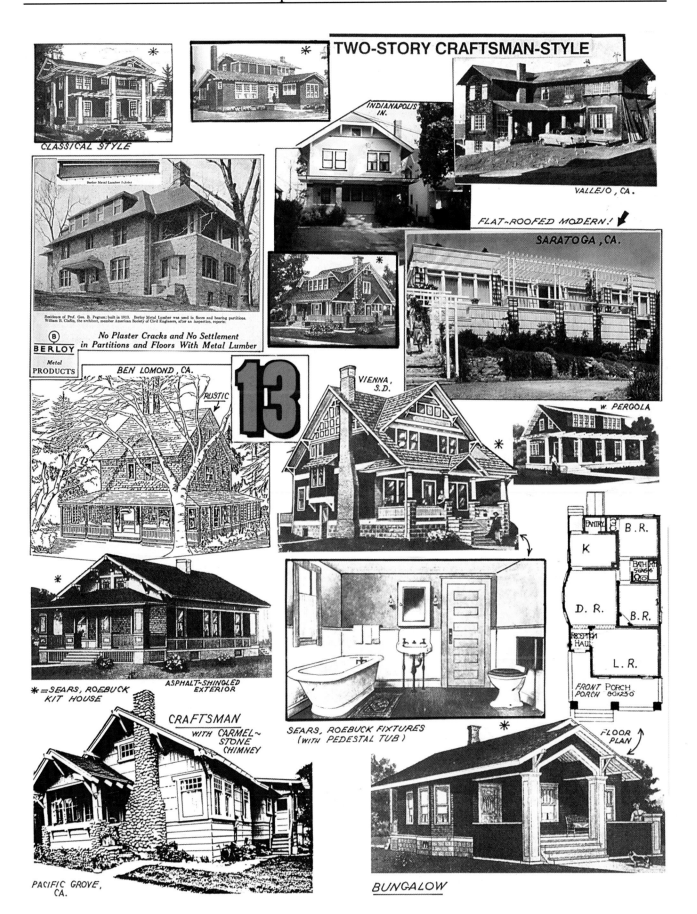

CLASSICAL STYLE

TWO-STORY CRAFTSMAN-STYLE

INDIANAPOLIS, IN.

VALLEJO, CA.

FLAT-ROOFED MODERN!

SARATOGA, CA.

Berloy Metal Lumber I-Joist

Residence of Prof. Geo. B. Pegram; built in 1913. Berloy Metal Lumber was used in floors and bearing partitions. William B. Claflin, the architect, member American Society of Civil Engineers, after an inspection, reports:

No Plaster Cracks and No Settlement in Partitions and Floors With Metal Lumber

(B) **BERLOY**
Metal
PRODUCTS

BEN LOMOND, CA.

RUSTIC

13

VIENNA, S.D.

W. PERGOLA

*=SEARS, ROEBUCK KIT HOUSE

ASPHALT-SHINGLED EXTERIOR

CRAFTSMAN WITH CARMEL~ STONE CHIMNEY

SEARS, ROEBUCK FIXTURES (WITH PEDESTAL TUB)

PANTRY

B.R.

K

BATH 56x60

D.R.

B.R.

RECEPTION HALL

L.R.

FRONT PORCH
PORCH 60x230

FLOOR PLAN

PACIFIC GROVE, CA.

BUNGALOW

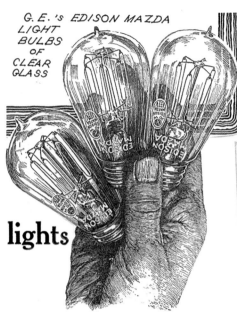

G.E.'s EDISON MAZDA LIGHT BULBS OF CLEAR GLASS

lights

13

The Hoosier

Saves Miles of Steps

PREFABRICATED KITCHEN CABINETS

The Noiselessness of the Siwelclo Is an Advantage Found in No Other Similar Fixture.

This appeals particularly to those whose sense of refinement is shocked by the noisy flushing of the old style closet. The Siwelclo was designed to prevent such embarrassment and has been welcomed whenever its noiseless feature has become known. When properly installed it cannot be heard outside of its immediate environment.

SIWELCLO Noiseless Siphon Jet CLOSET

Every sanitary feature has been perfected in the Siwelclo—deep water seal preventing the passage of sewer gas, thorough flushing, etc.

The Siwelclo is made of Trenton Potteries Co. Vitreous China, with a surface that actually repels dirt.

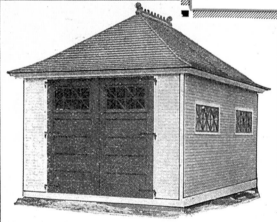

It is a money saver, a time saver, and a car saver. No nerve-trying waits to get your car from the garage; no excessive charges for storage and oil; no "unaccountable" breakages and attendant repair bills.

SPRINGFIELD PORTABLE GARAGES

KOHLER'S "BRISTOL" WASHOUT W.C. ABOUT TO BE DISCONTINUED AS OBSOLETE.

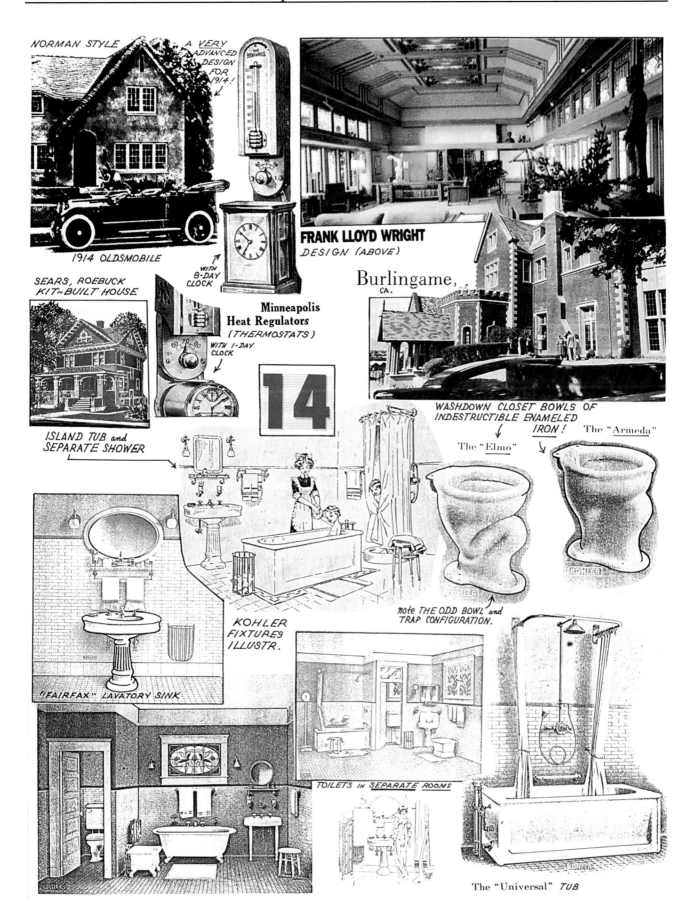

NORMAN STYLE
A VERY ADVANCED DESIGN FOR 1914!

1914 OLDSMOBILE

WITH 8-DAY CLOCK

SEARS, ROEBUCK KIT~BUILT HOUSE

Minneapolis Heat Regulators (THERMOSTATS)

WITH 1-DAY CLOCK

14

ISLAND TUB and SEPARATE SHOWER

FRANK LLOYD WRIGHT DESIGN (ABOVE)

Burlingame, CA.

WASHDOWN CLOSET BOWLS OF INDESTRUCTIBLE ENAMELED IRON!

The "Elmo"

The "Armeda"

note THE ODD BOWL and TRAP CONFIGURATION.

KOHLER FIXTURES ILLUSTR.

"FAIRFAX" LAVATORY SINK

TOILETS in SEPARATE ROOMS

The "Universal" TUB

The Popular Five-Room Bungalow

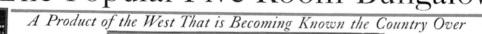

A Product of the West That is Becoming Known the Country Over

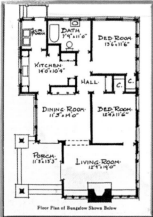

A TYPICAL SIDE STAIRWAY

VARIOUS NEWEL POSTS

CEMENT ON LOWER FRONT PORTION SHAKE SHINGLE SIDING

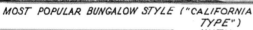

MOST POPULAR BUNGALOW STYLE ("CALIFORNIA TYPE") WITH LOW ROOFLINE

BRICK MIDWEST TYPE

100~ROOM "CAROLANDS" MANSION   Hillsborough, Ca.

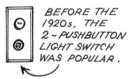

BEFORE THE 1920s, THE 2 ~ PUSHBUTTON LIGHT SWITCH WAS POPULAR.

French Windows

Ceiling Beams and Paneling

An artistic interior—using "CEIL-TITE" Wall Board

FRENCH WINDOW, 10-H-304.

FRENCH WINDOW, 10-H-305.

FRENCH WINDOW, 10-H-306.

15

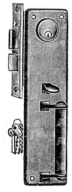

Bookcase Colonnade
(ROOM DIVIDER)

"FAN LIGHT" WINDOW OVER DOOR

WHITE CITY FRONT ENTRANCE
See Style BB for Prices of Frames.

COLONIAL FRONT ENTRANCE

Transom 10-E-407. Morning Glory Door. Sidelights 10-E-41

10-E-214 Sidelight.   Magnolia Door.

HARRIS BROTHERS COMPANY
35th and Iron Sts., Chicago.

CHICAGO FRONT ENTRANCE
See Style AA for Prices of Frames.

FRONT DOOR LATCH WITH HANDLE

BATHROOM

"Viceroy" Bath, Plate No. K-11½-A   "Filmore" Lavatory, Plate No. K-141-D

KOHLER manufactures but one quality of enameled plumbing ware of uniform color and only the highest grade.

AN ALADDIN KIT~BUILT HOUSE WINS SPECIAL AWARD AT THE 1915 WORLD'S FAIR, SAN FRANCISCO, FOLLOWING A MICHIGAN STATE FAIR AWARD IN 1914.

MAJESTIC BATHROOM OUTFIT

PRICE COMPLETE $37.50

MEDITERRANEAN

WHITE PLAINS, N.Y. → HIP ROOF

ELK-HART, IN.

FOLSOM, PA.

*Stucco Home
Folsom, Pa.
Amos Ellis, Architect*

Bay State Brick & Cement **Coating**

weatherproofs and gives concrete or stucco a lasting artistic effect in white or tint. "Bay State" has been proved by architects and home builders everywhere.

WESTERN

BUNGALOW

STUCCO HOUSES

Your Home

First Cost   Upkeep

Total $28663

CHATHAM, N.Y.

Kno-Burn
TRADE MARK
Expanded Metal Lath

construction with
NATCO·HOLLOW·TILE

PLAINFIELD, N.J.

16

"OLD WORLD" STYLES

MILWAUKEE, WI.

WILSON EYRE & McILVAINE   ... ECTS

FRONT and REAR VIEWS INTERIOR

Miami   ITALIAN STYLE MANSION

1916 COPPER ELEMENT

DAY and NIGHT WATER HEATER

(**NEW**)

1916 "CANDLESTICK" TELEPHONE

LEWIS-BUILT HOMES
DIRECT TO YOU CUTS COST IN TWO

Lewis Mfg. Co.
Dept. 267
Bay City, Mich.

The VALLEJO COMPLETE $1175

LARGE FRONT DORMER and WIDE FRONT PORCH POPULAR IN 1916.

The Hard Wear Varnish

PITCAIRN AGED VARNISH

FAMILY FUN

MONTAWK COMPLETE $895

Mazda Lamp

Home Inter-phone

Electric Lantern

Electric Toaster

Electric Iron

No. 11 Vacuum Cleaner "The Cleaner NOT Built Like a Broom"

Large Electric Vacuum Cleaner

Electric Washer and Wringer

1916 ELECTRICAL APPLIANCES

16

TRENTON "PEG LEG" PEDESTAL SINK

WASH TUBS and KITCHEN SINK (TRENTON)

MODERN GREENHOUSE   LUTTON CO.

TRENTON ROUND PEDESTAL SINK

The Trenton Potteries Co.
Bath Rooms of Character

Standard Sanitary Mfg. Co.   Pittsburgh

new 1916 "COMARINA" TUB ILLUSTR.

"Standard"

BUILT-IN BATHS help to lend that finer touch which identifies the well appointed home.

Homes

ECLECTIC "BOX" STYLE

"AUBURN"

SEARS, ROEBUCK KIT HOUSE 4 BEDRMS., 1 BATH

The New Kind of Color Stucco

DO YOU INTEND TO BUILD?

75 PRACTICAL PLANS

California Bungalows and Houses especially suited to any climate. New, attractive designs with valuable building suggestions all in handsome **1917 Art Plan Book. Price $1.00 postpaid.** Send today for your copy. Save time, trouble. Money refunded if not satisfactory. Address BUILDING DEPARTMENT **AURELIUS SWANSON COMPANY, Inc.**

PACIFIC GROVE, CALIF.

SHINGLES ON 2ND-STORY EXTERIOR

MONTEREY, CA.

BUNGALOWS

"DELEVAN" MODEL

SEARS, ROEBUCK KIT HOUSE (4 ROOMS)

K · BATH · B.R. · CLO. CLO. · B.R. · LIVING AND DINING ROOM · PORCH

PAIGE "The Most Beautiful Car in America"

1917 PAIGE PHAETON

BUTLER, KY.

Homes

STUCCO
MODIFIED
CAPE COD COLONIAL

PACIFIC GROVE, CALIF.
MIXED ELEMENTS of SOUTHERN
and MONTEREY COLONIAL STYLE

CATALOG
ORDERING

Buying Your Home

RUSTIC

PINK~STUCCO
NORMAN STYLE

WHITE
ATLAS
CEMENT

A CALIFORNIA BUNGALOW—WITH OUTDOOR ALL-YEAR LIVING ROOM.

UNUSUAL LOW~ROOFED REDWOOD CONSTRUCTION

(BELOW)
ADVANCE~DESIGN TRACT of HOMES, ALL
BUILT
WITH

MT. KISCO, N.Y.

Estimated cost $2800

SEATTLE

17 BUNGALOW
(2 TYPES)

LOS ANGELES

LOW ROOFLINE with COLUMNED FRONT PERGOLA ←

GROSSMONT, CALIF.

California Redwood
BUNGALOW INTERIOR (ABOVE)

RITE GRADE INSPECTED RED CEDAR SHINGLES

DUTCH COLONIALS

Sterling System Home

The Elms

Build in 1917! with RED CEDAR

CAMBRIDGE, MA. ←

PEDESTAL TUB

BUILT OF
NATCO·HOLLOW·TILE

"EDWARDIAN"
LOS ANGELES

Homes *of* Beauty

MANSIONS

17

MEDITERRANEAN

Bay State Coating Beautifies
and Protects Walls

Home of Chas. A. Nicola, 10900 Magnolian Avenue, Cleveland. Architect, J. W. C. Corbusier, Cleveland, Ohio.

CLEVELAND, OH.

Nemco Products

beauty of this dwelling:
stucco over metal lath

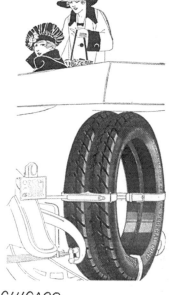

"*CHICAGO*
ECLECTIC "

KIT HOUSES

ALADDIN Homes

Ready-Cut Homes

548 Buys It

Montgomery Ward & Co.

New York   Chicago   Kansas City
Ft. Worth   Portland, Ore.

KIT = $1297.

$989 for this 7-Room Aladdin

HERE is your opportunity to own a home and dodge high building prices. You can do it even though building prices are going up! THE ALADDIN READI-CUT SYSTEM OF BUILDING stands between you and present high prices. It offers you this ideal home or one hundred other attractive homes at substantial savings in price. Think of the home pictured above containing large living room and dining room, large kitchen, grade cellar entrance, three large bedrooms, bathroom, closets and porch for $989.00 for complete material, readi-cut. This is only one of a hundred homes with prices from $200 to $8000 shown in the handsome book. Let us send you a copy of this book entitled "Aladdin Homes." Send stamps today for your copy.

Avoid High Building Prices   **Dollar-a-Knot Guarantee**   **Styles for Every Taste**

$1.00 DISCOUNT FOR EACH KNOTHOLE FOUND IN THE KIT WOOD

Dwellings, Bungalows, Summer Cottages, Garages

Aladdin Houses are erected the same as other houses. Aladdin Houses are cut-to-fit—no waste of lumber or labor. The Aladdin price includes all materials cut-to-fit as follows: Lumber, millwork, flooring, outside and inside finish, doors, windows, shingles, lath and plaster, hardware, locks, nails, paint, varnishes. The complete material is shipped to you in a sealed box car, complete, ready to erect. Safe arrival of the complete material in perfect condition is guaranteed. Send stamps today for a copy of "Aladdin Homes," No. 190.

The Aladdin Co.
"Homebuilders to the Nation"
666 Aladdin Ave., Bay City, Mich.

Parts $955

17

LEWIS MFG. CO., BAY CITY, MICH.

KIT: $814.

BUNGALOW

UNIVERSAL ELECTRIC HOME NEEDS

UNIVERSAL Electric Percolator No. E9635 $8.50

UNIVERSAL American-Sheffield Plate Electric Coffee Urn Colonial Loving Cup Pattern No. E8166 $22.50

UNIVERSAL Electric Toaster No. E946 $4.50

Lewis-Built Homes Solve the Problem

KITCHENS

A Convenient Kitchen

BURNS NATURAL or ARTIFICIAL **GAS** and **COAL or WOOD**

No Parts to Change

Women Need
UNIVERSAL
Portable Electric Range
No. E19684 $21.50

Ornamental Kitchen Sinks

Melville Roll Rim Sink
$20.10

Sink Only With Legs
$43.80
Windsor Deep Rim Sink

Novo Roll Rim Sink
$13.95

Sink Only With Legs
$49.10
Crescent Deep Rim Corner Sink

17

LAUNDRY ROOM

UNIVERSAL

ELECTRIC IRON

UNIVERSAL
Electric Four Heat Grill
No. E984 $6.50

new E-905 MODEL
$4.50

CARLTON DOUBLE TUB
$12.10

$17.85
Medford Triple Tub

Mosaic Floor Tile

Bathroom Tile

White Enameled Wall Tile

ESTABLISHED **MOTT** *1828*

MOTT

RUUD
AUTOMATIC GAS
WATER HEATER
"Hot Water"

17

QUIET-ACTION *Closets*

WHY install a noisy closet? Our Quiet-Action Closets effectively silence the rush—swish—hiss and gurgle of the flushing operation.

For sixteen years the SILENTIS—the pioneer quiet-action closet—has been furnished for the finest homes throughout America.

The SILENTUM insures the feature of quietness, and costs no more than an ordinary closet of a dependable grade.

There's Hot Water Ready if You Own a RUUD

RUUD
AUTOMATIC GAS
WATER HEATER

(AVAILABLE, BUT OLD-FASHIONED BY 1917) **High Tank Closet Combinations**

$19³⁵

$20⁴⁰

$17⁹⁵

73.00　　Colonial Bathroom Outfit　　$73.00

Ionia Syphon Wash-Down Closet

Marvin Syphon Jet Closet

Grimsby Frost-Proof Closet

PACIFIC GROVE, CA.

B.R. K BATH L.R. D.R. PORCH

⑤ = A SEARS ROEBUCK KIT HOUSE (OR A ROOM FROM)

4~ROOM BUNGALOW

AVAILABLE FOR PRIVATE RESIDENCES →

CAPE COD STYLE ↑

18

UP DOWN BATH B.R. K D.R. PORCH B.R. L.R. B.R.

Mueller Sanitary Drinking Fountains

4~BEDROOM HOME WITH HIPPED~GABLE ROOF

TYPICAL KITCHEN ⑤

WICKER FURNITURE POPULAR FOR SUN ROOMS, ETC.

1918 HUDSON

⑤

EARLY AMERICAN STYLE (RUSTIC)

BUILT OF **California Redwood** Resists rot and fire ↓

AVAIL. 1918 ONLY ↘

⑤

WASHINGTON, D.C.

2~STORY HOUSES

IN BALTIMORE, MD.

"CREO-DIPT" Stained Shingles

Panoramic view of part of George R. Morris' Development, Arlington, Baltimore, Md. "CREO-DIPT" Stained Shingles used on all these houses.

DAYTON, OH.

DUTCH COLONIAL with WIDE DORMER

MISSION STYLES

PITTSBURGH, PA.

"PRESTON" COLONIAL

18

CLASSIC STYLE

4 B.R. 2½ BA.

K

HALL

L.R.

D.R.

RECEPTN HALL

DOWN

SLEEPING PORCH

BEDROOM

B.R.

B.R.

HALL

BATH

B.R.

B.R.

UP

4 BEDROOMS 2½ BATHS

"MAGNOLIA" SEARS, ROEBUCK'S SHOWPIECE HOUSE OF 1918 $5140. and up (KIT)

COUNTRY HOUSE At PELHAM, N.Y.

REAR

NORMAN STYLE

RECEPTION HALL

MUELLER PLUMBING FIXTURES

H. MUELLER MFG. COMPANY, DECATUR, ILL.

(SINCE 1858)   (BELOW)

I~SPOUT LAVATORY SINK ➔

FORMAL DINING ROOM

90

BUNGALOWS
(KIT-BUILT)

Sterling System Home

COZY, ARTISTIC COTTAGE

SEATTLE

COLONIAL

The Classic
Net Price $1423.10

ROCKY RIVER, OH.

BEDROOM

ATTACHED GARAGE

2-FAMILY FLATS

FRONT PERGOLA

19

GOTHIC STYLE

Olde Stonesfield Roofs

Indiana Limestone WALLS

New Residence

Dodge Brothers 4-Door Sedan

FRENCH MANOR STYLE

A FRANK LLOYD WRIGHT DESIGN

MEDITERRANEAN

OAKLAND, CA.

LOS ANGELES

HUMPHREY
AUTOMATIC GAS WATER HEATER
Humphrey Company   Kalamazoo, Mich.

MEDITERRANEAN MANSION   NEAR LOS ANGELES

19

"OLD WORLD" STYLE
GREAT NECK, L.I., N.Y.

TURRET ENTRANCE ←

"OLDE ENGLISH" GOTHIC STYLE

NEWPORT, R.I.

SARGENT & COMPANY
Hardware Manufacturers
35 Water St., New Haven, Conn.

SARGENT

Noiseless Screen Door Closers

1919 STEEL ELEMENT

DAY and NIGHT WATER HEATER

The Choice of the Well-Informed

CRANE
LUXURY BATHROOM IN A MANSION

LAUNDRY ROOM

KITCHEN

"Standard" Plumbing   Fixtures

Chapter 5

1920-1929

European revival styles dominated this decade. Americans had become increasingly fascinated with European, especially British, culture and life, such as the activities of the royal family. This was reflected in the houses they chose to build: Tudor, Jacobethan Revival, and English Cottage Revival. These featured half-timbered walls, cross-hatched and small-pane casement windows, crenellated two-story bay windows, Dutch or Flemish gables (with walls that extended beyond their roof-planes), round-headed or slightly pointed (Tudor) arches, deep and layered doorways, fireplaces with large outside chimneys, and jerkin-head and rolled-shingle roofs (to imitate thatch).

Also becoming popular were Continental styles. French and Norman revivals had high-pitched hip or deck roofs and round towers with conical roofs. The Mediterranean style had flat tiled roofs with balustrades (railings), round-headed windows and doors, and wrought-iron balconies. Swiss-chalet copies were characterized by half-timbering, wide eaves, ornate wooden bargeboards (eave trim), and balconies. Even Moorish Revival houses could be found, with ogee (onion-shaped) arches, latticework, and ornate exterior mosaic-tile medallions.

Some houses from this period had brick exteriors, instead of the mostly wood of the Craftsman/Bungalow styles, and many had walls of stucco. Some of them also had an extended front wall to one side or the other, like a flying buttress, usually with a doorway or window, and frequently threaded by a sidewalk that ran along the side of the house.

Cultural changes during this period included gas kitchen-ranges, built-in (Murphy) beds and ironing boards, twin beds, metal kitchen and bathroom appliances, metal window frames and mullions, beaver board, hollow building tiles (for the frames of houses), awnings, French doors, glass doorknobs, and the proliferation of garages, many of them built in the same styles as their houses.

Kohler, Standard, and other manufacturers offered colored plumbing fixtures from 1928 on.

The Plaza

ALADDIN HOMES
"Built in a Day"

THE ALADDIN COMPANY
Home Offices, Bay City, Michigan

The Hudson

"POMONA"

BUNGALOWS

The Raymond

1ST FLOOR

2ND FLOOR

First Floor Plan The Hudson

Second Floor Plan—The Hudson

20 KIT HOUSES

The Oakley

The Detroit

THIS DESIGN MORE "DATED" THAN THE OTHERS. LOOKS 10~15 YEARS BEHIND THE TIMES!

The Edison

A MORE MODERN DESIGN

The Pasadena

The Sunshine BUNGALOW

The Jordan

Living Room— The Colonial

ALADDIN

Second Floor Plan The Colonial

The Colonial

RECEPT. HALL and STAIRWAY

(BRENT~ WOOD MODEL)

Reception Hall The Brentwood

2ND FLOOR

First Floor Plan—The Brentwood.

1ST FLOOR

The Shadow Lawn

BOOKCASES ON BOTH ENDS OF MANTEL ARE TYPICAL.

The Brentwood

KITCHEN CABINET

ALADDIN Bathroom Cabinet and Medicine Chest →

The Maxwell

The Buick Garage

The Winton

The Packard

The Peerless

ALADDIN GARAGES ARE NAMED FOR VARIOUS BRANDS OF AUTOMOBILES.

The Buick

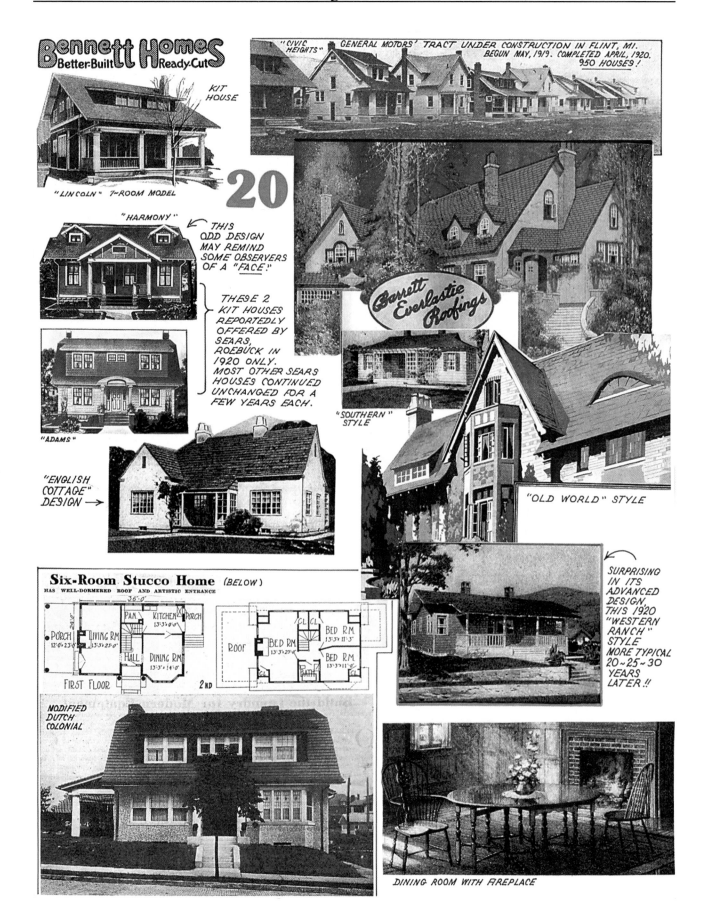

Bennett Homes Better-Built Ready-Cut

KIT HOUSE

"LINCOLN" 7-ROOM MODEL

"HARMONY"

← THIS ODD DESIGN MAY REMIND SOME OBSERVERS OF A "FACE."

THESE 2 KIT HOUSES REPORTEDLY OFFERED BY SEARS, ROEBUCK IN 1920 ONLY. MOST OTHER SEARS HOUSES CONTINUED UNCHANGED FOR A FEW YEARS EACH.

"ADAMS"

"ENGLISH COTTAGE" DESIGN →

"CIVIC HEIGHTS" GENERAL MOTORS' TRACT UNDER CONSTRUCTION IN FLINT, MI. BEGUN MAY, 1919. COMPLETED APRIL, 1920. 950 HOUSES!

20

Barrett Everlastic Roofings

"SOUTHERN" STYLE

"OLD WORLD" STYLE

SURPRISING IN ITS ADVANCED DESIGN THIS 1920 "WESTERN RANCH" STYLE MORE TYPICAL 20~25~30 YEARS LATER!!

Six-Room Stucco Home (BELOW)
HAS WELL-DORMERED ROOF AND ARTISTIC ENTRANCE

PORCH 12'-0"x23'-0" | LIVING RM. 13'-3"x23'-0" | PAN. | KITCHEN 13'-3"x0'-0" | PORCH | HALL | DINING RM. 13'-3"x14'-0"

FIRST FLOOR

ROOF | CL CL | BED RM. 13'-3"x11'-3" | BED RM. 13'-3"x23'-0" | BED RM. 13'-3"x11'-0" | BATH

2ND

MODIFIED DUTCH COLONIAL

DINING ROOM WITH FIREPLACE

NEW DEVELOPMENT IN SOUTHERN CALIFORNIA (BUNGALOWS IN RIGHT FOREGROUND)

21

2~STORY STUCCO URBAN AMERICAN ECLECTIC STYLE

CORVALLIS, OR.

LONG-BELL TRADE-MARKED LUMBER

KANSAS CITY, MO.

Bungalow

SWISS CHALET STYLE

SPANISH REVIVAL

LOS ANGELES   MEDITERRANEAN

"PITTSBURGH" WATER HEATER (note THE ORNATE STYLE OF THIS RARE 1921 "MUSEUM PIECE!")

ALADDIN KIT HOUSE

DAVENPORT, IA.

Home No.521—Seven-room, 1-story bungalow. Four bedrooms. Large kitchen, dining and living rooms. Big hall. Coat closet. Built-in conveniences. Attic. Fine bath. Large porch. Distinctive appearance. See catalog.

Rolling Screen

Rolup SCREEN

SHINGLED EXTERIORS

Moderate Sized Residence

SEATTLE

of HOLLOW TILE CONSTRUCTION

CHICAGO

—Indiana Limestone embodies all the essentials of a good building material, and may be obtained in the following shades: Buff, Gray and Variegated.

MINNEAPOLIS, MN.

MANHASSET, L.I. N.Y.

21 Stucco

FRENCH MANOR STYLES

IN HAVERFORD, PA.

RES. W. G. STUBER (WILLOW BANK) ROCHESTER N.Y.

ARCH. J. FOSTER WARNER ROCHESTER N.Y.

BISHOPRIC USED ON EXTERIORS & INTERIORS

ROCHESTER, N.Y.

HOLLOW TILE CONSTRUCTION

FIRST FLOOR

GARAGE

KITCHEN

DINING ROOM

HALL

LIVING ROOM

PORCH

SECOND FLOOR

BEDROOM

HALL

BEDROOM

BEDROOM

CLOS.

SPRINGFIELD, OH.

EARLY AMERICAN COLONIAL STYLE

21

DUTCH COLONIAL and FLOOR PLAN

convenience receptacle

A QUAINT COTTAGE ENTRY

LOCK

HANDLE

Sargent Door Closers

Sargent Door Closers keep the doors closed that should be closed. Not only the screen door, but the kitchen, bathroom, back stair and other doors, light or heavy, inside or out. The absence of slam-bang adds to the restfulness of your home.

hardware

BUILD NOW

And let Sargent Hardware add the final touch of beauty and security to your home.

AWNINGS POPULAR

Danger!

Safety!

Square D Safety Switch
ON
OFF

Important New Ruling of National Board of Fire Underwriters—effective January 1st, 1921.

"The service switch must be enclosed and preferably of a type that may be operated without exposing the live parts to accidental contact. Service switches must indicate plainly whether they are open or closed."

G-E TWIN RECEPTACLE

artistic *Stucco*

Square D Safety Switch
Makes Electricity Safe for Everyone

NORMAN / OLDE ENGLISH COTTAGE STYLE

TUDOR

CLASSIC STYLE

NEW ROCHELLE, N.Y.

EARLY AMERICAN

SHINGLES, since Colonial days, have been used on side walls.

22

BUNGALOW

VARIOUS COLORS OF BRICK

MOORISH-STYLE INTERIOR

HOUSE 15 YRS. OLD WHEN THIS 1937 PHOTO TAKEN. NOTE 1929-ERA CONSOLE RADIO.

PITTSBURGH, PA.

RUMSON, N.J.

KIT AVAIL. FROM SEARS, ROEBUCK

INTERIOR

COLONIAL (BRICK)

CONTINUED POPULARITY OF DUTCH COLONIAL STYLE

A·F·B·A USE FACE BRICK —it Pays

DOWN

FLOOR PLAN

UP

HEARTH

SOUTHERN~STYLE BUNGALOW

FOLD~OUT MURPHY BED CONCEALED IN CLOSET

1922 UNIVERSAL GAS RANGE

HOT WATER HEAT RADIATOR ←

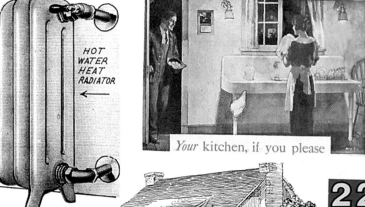

Your kitchen, if you please

22

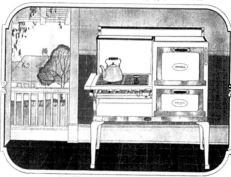

CRANE

CRANE

BATHROOMS and FIXTURES

KOHLER

BUNGALOWS

STUCCO OVER HOLLOW TILE

FLOOR PLAN

FLOOR PLAN

23

DINING ROOM

DUPLEX

RUSTIC COTTAGE

COLONIAL

SHINGLED and STUCCO EXTERIOR

PROVINCIAL STYLE

BERKELEY, CA.

EXTERIOR and INTERIOR VIEWS

LIVING ROOM

BURLINGAME, CA.

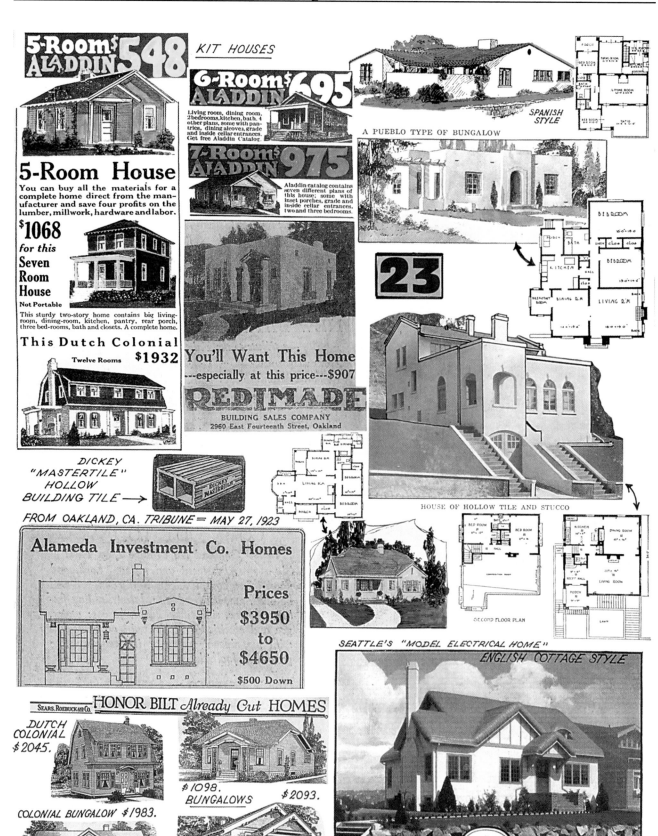

5-Room $548 ALADDIN

KIT HOUSES

6-Room $695 ALADDIN

Living room, dining room, 2 bedrooms, kitchen, bath. 4 other plans, some with pantries, dining alcoves, grade and inside cellar entrances. Get free Aladdin Catalog.

7-Room $975 ALADDIN

Aladdin catalog contains seven different plans of this house; some with inset porches, grade and inside cellar entrances, two and three bedrooms.

5-Room House

You can buy all the materials for a complete home direct from the manufacturer and save four profits on the lumber, millwork, hardware and labor.

$1068
for this
Seven Room House
Not Portable

This sturdy two-story home contains big living-room, dining-room, kitchen, pantry, rear porch, three bed-rooms, bath and closets. A complete home.

This Dutch Colonial
Twelve Rooms **$1932**

You'll Want This Home
---especially at this price---$907

REDIMADE
BUILDING SALES COMPANY
2960 East Fourteenth Street, Oakland

SPANISH STYLE

A PUEBLO TYPE OF BUNGALOW

23

HOUSE OF HOLLOW TILE AND STUCCO

DICKEY "MASTERTILE" HOLLOW BUILDING TILE →

DICKEY MASTERTILE

FROM OAKLAND, CA. TRIBUNE = MAY 27, 1923

Alameda Investment Co. Homes

Prices
$3950
to
$4650

$500 Down

SECOND FLOOR PLAN

SEATTLE'S "MODEL ELECTRICAL HOME"
ENGLISH COTTAGE STYLE

SEARS, ROEBUCK AND CO. HONOR BILT *Already Cut* **HOMES**

DUTCH COLONIAL $2045.

$1098. BUNGALOWS $2093.

COLONIAL BUNGALOW $1983.

WATERPROOFED WHITE MEANS **MEDUSA**

Medusa Stainless White Cement-   -Plain and waterproofed

CENTS—SUNDAY TEN CENTS   OAKLAND, CALIFORNIA, SUNDAY, SEPTEMBER 9, 1923.

New Maxwell Park "Show House"

More than 3000 people visited the "show-home" in Maxwell since it was opened to the public, according to J. H. A. Shealey, sales-manager for Burritt & Shealey, pioneer builders in Maxwell Park. The house, an American adaption of French architecture, is situated on the corner of Fleming avenue and Rawson street, in the central of Maxwell Park.

The interior arrangement, considered from the viewpoint of the busy housewife, is compact and convenient. An inviting entrance begs the visitor to enter a spacious living room. Long French windows grace the side facing Rawson street, while a beautiful fireplace and two book-cases adorn the east side of this room. French doors connect the living room with the dining room and the dining room with a large front porch. A low buffet of "Morgan" pattern completes the picture. The kitchen is located in the central part of the house with a delightful breakfast room on one side and the rear entrance and laundry on the other. Large kitchen cabinets, cooler and tile drainboards help to make work in this kitchen a pleasure.

Features especially appreciated by discriminating home-seekers are the large closets, abundant windows and the many built-in cases and cabinets, too numerous to mention.

The house is furnished by the Breuner Furniture company. The kitchen stove, water heater, fixtures utensils are supplied by the Maxwell Hardware, company.

Burritt & Shealey have completed this sample home in Maxwell Park for the purpose of demonstrating their work. The home is completely furnished, and shows just how a residence of that size should be arranged. The Breuner Company supplies the furnishings and the Maxwell Company the stoves and kitchen supplies.

Maxwell Park Homes Must Be Different

Looking over Maxwell Park from the new office of Burritt & Shealey, who are putting up a new unit of fifty homes in this tract. Building in Maxwell Park was never more active than now. Individual lot owners are building in addition to the Burritt & Shealey activity. Photo by Ford E. Samuel.

5-20-23 OAK TRIB
TRACT UNDER CONSTRUCTION
OAKLAND, CA.

THOUGH IN WORN CONDITION, THESE ORIGINAL NEWS CLIPPINGS ARE TOO RARE AND IMPORTANT NOT TO INCLUDE!

SEPTEMBER 7, 1923
LOTS FOR SALE—Continued.   40—LOTS FOR SALE—Continued

take the Arlington D'car to—
BERKELEY HIGHLANDS
and gaze on the scene below.

Entrance to Tract

Oakland Tribune
United Press   International News Service

OAKLAND, CALIFORNIA, WEDNESDAY EVENING, MAY 20, 1923

...AVE BEEN MADE IN REAL ESTATE

(By B. S. Sanders, for the Oakland Real Estate Board)

New Homes 23

One of the new homes in Berkeley Highlands, adjoining Kensington Park at the Arlington car line, Berkeley.—Courtesy of Myran Bros.

BERKELEY HIGHLANDS, BERKELEY, CA.

Development

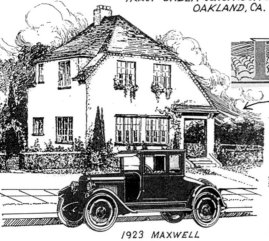

1923 MAXWELL

Interior Arrangement.

DOWNSTAIRS
- PANTRY
- KITCHEN 13'-6" x 9'-0"
- COATS
- HALL
- LIVING AND DINING ROOM 21'-0" x 15'-0"
- PORCH 7'-6" x 13'-0"
- 30'-0"

UPSTAIRS
- LINEN
- BATH
- HALL
- SEWING RM. 7'-0" x 5'-0"
- BED ROOM 12'-9" x 12'-6"
- BED ROOM 11'-9" x 12'-6"

ENGLISH STYLE WITH TURRET

BUILD THE NATION SECURELY

COLONIAL

BUNGALOWCRAFT

ENGLISH STYLE

24

"CREO-DIPT"

Stained Shingles
NORTH~EASTERN STYLE

Cincinnati home

SOUTHERN STYLE

DUTCH COLONIAL

ELMSFORD, N.Y.

FARM STYLE

WAUSAU, WIS.

RUSSWIN
DISTINCTIVE HARDWARE

BRICK INTERIOR

"ROOSEVELT" STYLE DOOR HARDWARE

KOHLER FIXTURES

SARGENT
Locks & Hardware

1924 SPIRAL FLUE (PATENTED)
DAY and NIGHT

LOS ANGELES

TYPICAL KITCHEN SCENE

ROPER
Complete Oven Control

Care-free Home Cooking ROPER

SPANISH STYLE

EXTENDING OUR HOUSES TO THE OUT-OF-DOORS
San Diego, Cal.
Meade & Requa Architects

FIRST FLOOR PLAN

MOORISH STYLE

"CALIFORNIA BUNGALOWS"

PLANS   BOOKS

CLASSICAL STYLE

24

PUEBLO STYLE (or "AZTEC")

EUROPEAN STYLE

PATIO
BED RM.
KITCHEN
PERGOLA
BATH
DINING RM.
BED RM.
LIVING RM.
VEST.
TERRACE
FIRST FLOOR PLAN

"The strength of a nation is in the homes of the people."—Mrs. Sigourney

GARAGE MATCHES STYLE OF HOUSE

CRANE

46'0"
BED ROOM 14'0"x11'0"   BED ROOM 14'0"x11'0"
LIVING RM. 14'6"x18'6"
28'0"   BATH RM.
PORCH   KITCHEN 11'6"x10'6"   DINING RM. 14'0"x15'6"   VEST.   PORCH
PANT   CLOS.
FLOOR PLAN   DRIVE WAY

LEHIGH CEMENT

VERY MODERN NORMAN STYLE

ISLAND TUB SET IN TILE BLACK DRESSING and SINK COUNTERS

(1924 WAS A COMPARITIVE-LY "SLOW" RECESSION YEAR, NOT EQUALING THE BIG CONSTRUCTION "BOOM" OF 1923 OR OF 1925.)

TOPEKA, KS.

1924 STUTZ

1925 WAS A BANNER YEAR FOR NEW CONSTRUCTION THROUGHOUT THE U.S.A.! THEREFORE, ADDITIONAL COVERAGE FOR 1925 HERE.

25

OKLAHOMA CITY YELLOW BRICK TUDOR/NORMAN STYLE

BETTER GRADE OF HOUSES

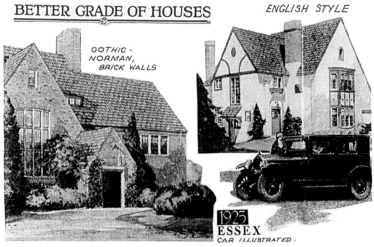

GOTHIC-NORMAN, BRICK WALLS

ENGLISH STYLE

1925 ESSEX CAR ILLUSTRATED.

(BELOW) HALF-TIMBERED TUDOR

AMERICAN ADAPTATION OF ENGLISH COTTAGE STYLE

For the first time —

a "thatch" roof at moderate cost

(RICHARDSON SHINGLES)

Now comes *the* onyx *roof*

COLORFUL COMPOSITION SHINGLES AVAILABLE

especially attractive on homes of yellow or white

FRAME EXTERIOR

COLONIAL VARIATIONS

KIT~BUILT

DUTCH COLONIAL (GAMBREL ROOF)

The PILGRIM

LEWIS MANUFACTURING CO.
Dept. C, Bay City, Mich.
EST. 1894 (100 DIFF. MODELS AVAIL.)

COLONIAL

WOOD~FRAME CONSTRUCTION DETAIL

NEW ENGLAND COLONIAL (IN FLUSHING, L.I., N.Y.)

Residence of W. T. Stokes, Corsicana, Texas. H. O. Blanding, Architect.

SOUTHWESTERN COLONIAL VARIATION (IN CORSICANA, TEXAS)

SHINGLED EXTERIORS

25

DESCRIBED AS A 6~RM. HOUSE, BUT APPEARS LARGER!

A~F~D~A USE FACE BRICK —It Pays

SECOND FLOOR

FACE BRICK EXT.

THIS TYPE OFTEN SEEN IN MID~AMERICA

SOUTHEASTERN COLONIAL

"NORMAN~ COLONIAL"

BUNGALOWS

LOW TAR-AND-GRAVEL ROOF

CARSON ROAD, FROM WILSHIRE BLVD. NORTH

(ABOVE) LOS ANGELES' WILSHIRE~BEVERLY HILLS TRACT OF PACIFIC READY-CUT MANUFACTURED KIT HOUSES (51 in ALL)

Entire Tracts Have Been Developed with Pacific Homes.

4 PACIFIC READY-CUT HOUSES FOR AN OIL CO. in L.A. AREA

RUSTIC BUNGALOW WITH FRENCH FRONT DOOR

SHINGLED ROOF

25

CORNER ENTRANCE WITH FRONT STOOP

DUPLEX

CLAPBOARD, DUAL PORCHES

Drop Ceiling

BATH BATH

DRESSING CLOS. DRESSING CLOS.

BEDCLOS. BEDCLOS.

LIVING ROOM 15'6"x 10' LIVING ROOM 15'6"x 10'

French Door French Door

PORCH

BUNGALOW DUPLEX and FLOOR PLAN

LOS ANGELES-STYLE FRAME BUNGALOW

note 2 VARIATIONS ON A SINGLE STYLE

FOR PLUMBING ECONOMY, KITCHEN and BATH OFTEN NEAR EACH OTHER

DETACHED GARAGE (THIS 2-CAR SIZE NOT COMMON IN 1925)

BUNGALOWS

BED ROOM

BED ROOM BATH HALL

BED ROOM

LIVING ROOM DINING ROOM

PORCH

BED ROOM

KITCHEN DINING ROOM

HALL

BATH LIVING ROOM

BED ROOM

TERRACE Cement Floor

BATH BETWEEN 2 BEDROOMS VERY POPULAR PLAN IN MID-1920s.

ON S. HILL ST., LOS ANGELES

COTTAGE STYLES

DARK, ROUGH-FINISHED STUCCO STILL USED ON SOME HOUSES

DUPLEX

WESTERN COTTAGES

STUCCO

FRAME

25

THIS 1925 DESIGN LOOKED 20 YRS. AHEAD OF ITS TIME!

STYLES LIKE THE 2 ABOVE WERE STILL POPULAR UNTIL MID~1930s.

BUNGALOW COTTAGE

THIS HOUSE A NEAR "MIRROR-TWIN" TO A SOUTHERN CALIFORNIA HOME WHICH WAS USED IN THE 1929 LAUREL and HARDY FILM COMEDY: "A PERFECT DAY."

TYPICAL OF THIS ERA, A FULLY-CONNECTING BATH WITH DOORWAYS TO 2 ADJOINING BEDROOMS BUT NOT TO ANY CORRIDOR

Style 204—Pacific Ready-Cut Court, Single Units   CALIF. MEDITERRANEAN

2-STORY DUPLEX

ITALIAN, STUCCO

AZTEC and MEDITER-RANEAN STYLES

Style 208—Court Unit   Style 209—2-Story Court Unit   Style 208—Court Unit

25

MEDITERRANEAN, STUCCO

4-FAMILY FLATS

AZTEC

Style 210—Court Unit   Style 211—2-Story Court Unit   Style 210—Court Unit

MISSION~ AZTEC

SINGLE FAMILY MEDITERRANEAN~ SPANISH

IN LONG BEACH, CALIF.

Style 212—Pacific Ready-Cut Court, Double Units

ABOVE = VARIOUS BUNGALOW COURTS, USING PACIFIC READY-CUT UNITS

(FREE-STANDING) AZTEC-STYLE BUNGALOW COURT UNIT

CALIFORNIA MOORISH with AUTOMOBILE GATE

ORNAMENTAL PLASTER DECORATIONS POPULAR IN 1925.

★ (MOST STRUCTURES ON THIS PAGE WERE AVAILABLE IN 1925, IN PRE-FABRICATED KIT FORM, FROM PACIFIC READY-CUT HOMES, LOS ANGELES.)

DUPLEX and FLOOR PLAN

BED ROOM   BATH   BATH   BED ROOM

CLOS.   CLOS.

HALL   HALL

KITCHEN   KITCHEN

DINING ROOM   DINING ROOM

LIVING ROOM   LIVING ROOM

TERRACE   ENTRY   ENTRY

★ EXCEPT FOR THE SINGLE-FAMILY MEDITERRANEAN~ SPANISH IN LONG BEACH, CALIF.

THIS STYLE SOMETIMES LOOSELY CLASSIFIED AS "MEDITERRANEAN"

SINGLE-FAMILY HOME   CALIFORNIA NORMAN, STUCCO

"SPANISH~ AZTEC"

GOOD TASTE IS EVIDENT IN THIS HOME OF C. C. SMITH, ESQ., WINDMILL POINTE, DETROIT WHERE LUPTON WINDOWS ARE USED THROUGHOUT

BRICK GOTHIC TUDOR MANOR HOUSE
IN DETROIT, MICH. AREA

Fenestra ~ ~
STEEL
Casement Windows

THESE TYPES
OF STEEL
CASEMENT
WINDOWS IN
USE UNTIL C. 1954

25

TUDOR

BEFORE and AFTER COMPLETION

DUPLEX

New With Six Cylinders OVERLAND CAR

APARTMENT HOUSE

NEW ENGLANDER STONE and FRAME STYLE

"AMERICAN ORIENTAL" STYLE with MATCHING GARAGE

SHEET STEEL CONSTRUCTION

Genasco Latite **Shingles**

Reg. U.S. Pat. Off.

The Barber Asphalt Company, Philadelphia

LATITE

VARIOUS TYPES

NORTHWESTERN NORMAN STYLE, LARGE, WITH DET. GARAGE

SEARS

Honor Bilt

OLDER ECLECTIC STYLES AVAIL. IN KIT HOUSES DURING 1920s.

25

NEW ENGLAND STYLE, SHINGLED WALLS

NORMAN AMERICAN STYLE IN MINNEAPOLIS

1925 LINCOLN

THIS LUXURIOUS MANSION MAKES EXTENSIVE USE OF DECORATIVE TILE, ALSO SHOWS INFLUENCE OF FRANK LLOYD WRIGHT'S EARLIER "PRAIRIE STYLE."

INTERNATIONAL STYLE IN SAN JUAN, PUERTO RICO

STUCCO

2~CAR

PUEBLO-AZTEC-SPANISH-
MEDITERRANEAN
STYLES

NORMAN
STYLES

STUCCO

GARAGES

ECLECTIC ★

COTTAGE
STYLE

★

VARIOUS
WOODEN
GARAGES

2~CAR

COLONIAL

"RED-
BARN"
STYLE

CAPE
COD

RUSTIC STYLE
(NATURAL WOOD)

(ABOVE, and LEFT ══)
A FEW PACIFIC "READY~CUT" GARAGES.
THOSE MARKED WITH A STAR (★)
WERE ON DISPLAY IN 1925,
AT 1330 S. HILL ST.,
LOS ANGELES,
CALIF.

ESTATE
"HEATROLA"

25

WALL THERMOSTAT →

The "MINNEAPOLIS"
HEAT REGULATOR
for COAL ~ GAS ~ OIL

A
NEIGHBORHOOD
OF
HOMES IN
ST. LOUIS,
MISSOURI

KEEP FLUES
CLEAN

KEEP FLUES
CLEAN

CAPITOL
WINCHESTER

CLINKER
DOOR

UNITED STATES RADIATOR
CORPORATION

CAPITOL
BOILER
(COAL-
FIRED)

Modern Heating Comfort

A
HEATER, DISGUISED AS A
PHONOGRAPH!
" There is only one Heatrola "
(SINCE 1921)

INTERIOR DETAILS

LIVING ROOM

MANTELS

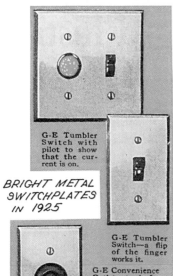

G-E Tumbler Switch with pilot to show that the current is on.

BRIGHT METAL SWITCHPLATES IN 1925

G-E Tumbler Switch—a flip of the finger works it.

G-E Convenience Outlets sturdy for service. Plenty of outlets mean real convenience.

PANELED DOOR

25

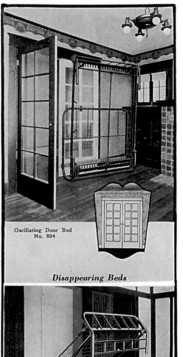

Oscillating Door Bed No. 804

Disappearing Beds

BUILT-IN BUFFET/BOOKCASE (OAK)

BUILT-IN IRONING BOARDS FOUND IN MANY HOUSES UNTIL 1940s.

SPICE CABINET OVER THE KITCHEN SINK (BELOW)

BUILT-IN BREAKFAST NOOKS

BATHROOMS

"CORWITH" TUB

CRANE BEAUTY IN THE OPEN; CRANE QUALITY IN ALL HIDDEN FITTINGS

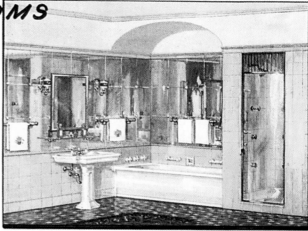

CRANE LUXURY BATHROOM and SHOWER STALL
"ELEGIA" SINK   "LINOVA" TUB

CRANE

CRANE BEAUTY

LUXURIOUS CRANE "NEUMAR"
LAVATORY SINK of BLACK ITALIAN
MARBLE, GOLD-VEINED, with
GOLD-PLATED LEGS and FITTINGS

KOHLER of KOHLER PEDESTAL SINK and TUB

MADDOCK

The
Maderno

The
Madbury

Why vitreous china

Vitreous china does not require constant scouring. It will always retain its snowy, glistening whiteness. Soil does not cling to it. It does not become roughened by use. It will not chip, split, crack nor stain; even acids cannot harm it.

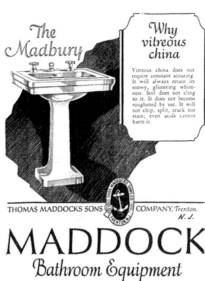

THOMAS MADDOCKS SONS COMPANY, Trenton, N.J.

MADDOCK
Bathroom Equipment

25

The Ariston
Madera Silent

BOILER
and
HEATER
COMBINATION

AVAIL. FROM PACIFIC "READY-CUT" HOMES

MISC.

BOSSERT KIT HOUSE ←

The Home of Your Dreams

THE "Piping Rock," a Bossert Bungalow Model, is famous throughout the country as the Blue Ribbon winner among bungalows. As an all-year-round home, guest house or summer bungalow, the "Piping Rock" is ideal.

"Ready Cut"
$1213
"Sectional"
$2205
F.O.B. Brooklyn

25

UNDER CONSTRUCTION

1½ STORY COUNTRY-STYLE BUNGALOWS ↗

A home at Rockford, Ill.
Designed by the Bliss Design Co.

SHINGLED EXTERIOR
(IN ROCKFORD, ILL.)

WASH TUB, SINK, DRAINBOARD and REMOVABLE COVER

1. Turn any hot water faucet

2. Gas valve is automatically opened

DETAILS OF THE HOFFMAN INSTANTANEOUS AUTOMATIC WATER HEATER

3. A tiny pilot ignites battery of burners

4. Steaming stream of hot water flows

What is a "sun porch" anyway?

IT'S ALSO KNOWN AS A "SUN ROOM" OR "SOLARIUM."

Two New Models
for Average Homes

—the No. 45 for small homes $90
—the No. 3, a larger model $125

THE HOFFMAN HEATER COMPANY,
Lorain, Ohio

CELTIC STYLE

Redwood

stucco tudor

DETROIT, MI.

Fenestra Casement Windows

SEATTLE

NORTHWESTERN STYLE

BETTER PLASTERING
ON METAL LATH

ORIENTAL STYLE

BIRMINGHAM, ALABAMA

26

BEAVER BOARD
INTERIOR WALLS
(NOT IN
ILLUSTRATED
HOUSES)

YOUNGSTOWN,
OH.
(ABOVE)

"Better Home" Exhibition House, Birmingham, Alabama. Built of limestone, backed with hollow tile, making fourteen-inch walls, absolutely solid, thoroughly fire-proof—Frank Hartley Anderson, Architect

ORIENTAL STUCCO

MEDITERRANEAN

A FEATURED HOME IN
SUNSET MAGAZINE,
EARLY 1927.

OAKLAND, CA.

RUSTIC

SHERMAN, TX.

BUILT-IN CHINA CLOSET IN CORNER

LINOLEUM TYPES

The Modern American house is much less formal in style than the only other American architectural expression—the Colonial.

Sun Parlors Are Modern American

ELGIN, IL.

PINEHURST, N.C.

COLONIAL

26

LUPTON STEEL CASEMENT WINDOWS

"MUSIC BOX COTTAGE" OMAHA, NE.

Square Handle
Toggle Switch
88

A new receptacle –
(AVAIL. LATER IN YEAR)
Rectangular Outlets
WITH BAKELITE SCREWLESS PLATES

WITH the receptacle completely hidden by the molded Bakelite flush plate, with no screws nor visible fastenings to detract from its handsome appearance, this Hubbell Rectangular Outlet is indeed "a new note of character in wall outlets." a new plate –

NO. 8791
METAL TYPE ALSO CONTINUES

HUBBELL
REG. U.S. PAT. OFF.

DUAL

HUBBELL

Good Hardware

CORBIN

MINNEAPOLIS
HEAT REGULATOR
COAL–GAS–OIL

THE MINNEAPOLIS
100
90
80
70
60
50

60 70 80

MINNEAPOLIS-77
SEVEN JEWEL

26

Honeywell

THERMO~
STATS

2524

2508   2510   2508

2549   2549

2523

2511   2511

2550

Prices of Riddle Fit do not include la...

Knob 1984

Handle 3961

HONEYWELL HEATING SPECIALTIES CO
Wabash, Indiana

EDWARD N. RIDDLE COMPANY, TOLEDO, OHIO

Riddle

SARGENT
LOCKS AND HARDWARE

Type R—New 15-20 day thermostat equipped with dependable jewelled-balance movement clock and high-grade thermometer.

KITCHEN MAID
STANDARD KITCHEN UNITS

GM ELECTRIC FRIGIDAIRE IN STEEL CABINET →

KITCHENS and BATHS

"STANDARD" FIXTURES

Seeger
WOODEN-CABINET REFRIGERATOR

Speakman H052½ Mixometer Shower and Deshler Bath Fixture over a built-in tub. The combination is the H 3370. The Lavatory Fixture is the Unit-Acto.

26

COVER UP THE SHOWER —
—and the Bathroom Seems Incomplete

⟦ *The bathroom is incomplete without a shower—it is the modern touch* ⟧

—But you want to make sure that your shower itself is modern.

The Speakman Company has developed and manufactured showers for the last twenty-five years of the fifty-seven years which we have been identified with the plumbing industry.

BUNGALOW

ENGLISH STYLE

VERY MODERN FOR 1927!

MEDITERRANEAN

NORMAN or CONTINENTAL

VIEW OF LIVING ROOM SHOWING FIREPLACE

TILED KITCHEN

27

Kitchen Maid Standard Unit

WALKER
SUPER-SINK
DISHWASHER

Compact, convenient sink

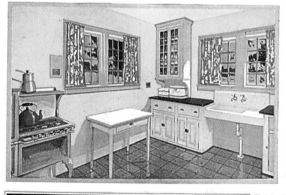

TUDOR

Kitchen Maid Pulmanook in special alcove. The Pulmanook with two chairs instead of four may be installed in a corner of the room. A special Dinette Pulmanook is designed for use on one wall space.

BREAKFAST NOOK

A New Idea

KOHLER FIXTURES
IN
COLOR

NEW

ABOVE AD APPEARED IN 12-3-27 SATURDAY
EVENING POST, WITH KOHLER FIXTURES AVAIL. IN
BLUE, GREEN, IVORY, BROWN, LAVENDER,
GRAY, OR
WHITE.

TILED BATH

A Combination Bath Tub

Regular Bath,
Seat Bath,
Shower Bath,
Foot Bath,
and
Child's Bath,
all in
one piece

ONE SIZE ONLY,
FOR ALL SIZE
PEOPLE

Sold through jobbers
of Plumbing Supplies

CRANE

CRANE

The Doris bath on legs

27

NEVADA

CRANE

ILLINI

CRANE

NOVA
CRANE

"ILLINI" HAS LG.
RECTANGULAR
TRAPWAY.
1929
"OKALOMA"
MODEL
SIMILAR.

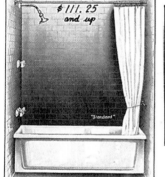

$111.25
and up

Recona Bath with Shower P 2481 B
Patented January 7, 1913, November 11, 1913

"Standard"

Essex Bath— $62.95
and up

$80.75   Essex Bath on Base—

$62.95

MOST
MFRS.
STILL
OFFERED
CLAW~
FOOT
TUBS
AS
THEIR
LOWEST~
PRICED
MODELS

New and Economical Bowl Features

"Standard"

EJECTO

$55.

**Cross Section of
Ejecto Closet,
F 2238**

👁 ← 1928~1929 "EJECTO" HAS ASSIST JET
ADDED, LOW IN TRAPWAY.

$70.

Expulso—F 2228

"Standard"
EXPULSO

Top View of
Expulso Bowl,
showing ingeni-
ous curved chan-
nel.

$100.

"Standard"
PURIMO

Top View of
Purimo Bowl.
Note Sanitary
Lip Feature —
Front and Back

China
LAVATORY SINK

B Handle

China
Lever
Handle

Anglo—

CORNER LAVATORY SINK $26.90
and up

"Standard"

"Standard"
PLUMBING FIXTURES

NEW

"TEMPLETON"
IS STANDARD'S
NEW TOP~LINE
LAVATORY
SINK.
(PEDESTAL and
WALL~HUNG
SINKS CONTINUE
AS USUAL.)

SCARBORO, N.Y.

prize design

GARAGE

SERVICE COURT

DINING RM.

KITCHEN

LIVING ROOM

HALL

LIBRARY

FIRST FLOOR PLAN →

OLDE ENGLISH STYLE

CLOSER DETAIL OF HOUSE AT TOP LEFT

HUTCHINSON, KS.

Photo by Charles Alma Byers

28

NORMAN STYLE

MOORISH

SPANISH/MED.

BEVERLY HILLS, CA.

MEDITERRANEAN

1928 CHRYSLER "62"

PACIFIC GROVE CA.

TWIN HOUSES BUILT IN 1928

SAN FRANCISCO 1928-A

COTTAGE STYLE

SPANISH~
MEDITER~
RANEAN
STYLES

29

SAN
FRANCISCO

DECORATIVE LAMP
(BY FRONT DOOR
OR GATE)
BY SMYSER~ROYER

ULTRA~MODERN/FUTURISTIC!

LOS ANGELES HILLS

1929
SIX CYLINDER SEDAN
$785
DESIGNED
BY
RICHARD
NEUTRA

Whippet
FOURS SIXES

MUELLER

BATH IN ABOVE HOUSE

SPEAKMAN SINK
FAUCET

Design Patent applied for.

The new Diamond sink fixture
with swing-nozzle, also in
Speakman Chromium Plate.

life-time metal!

For that atmosphere
of charm, select Sanitas
WALLPAPER

MONEL METAL
MODERN AS TOMORROW
easily-cleaned

1929~B

Chapter 6

1930-1939

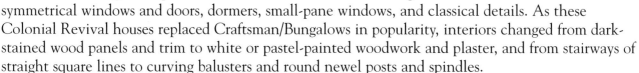

Two major themes characterize the decade of the Great Depression: One looking back to the past for our styles, and the other looking into the future.

The Colonial Revival featured styles that were popular in America before 1800. As we have seen, the earliest New England houses had asymmetrical gables, crosshatched casement windows, a garrison (second-story) overhang, and a large central chimney. Federal houses had gabled single-ridgepole roofs. Georgian houses had rectangular hip or deck roofs. Most Federal and Georgian houses had symmetrical windows and doors, dormers, small-pane windows, and classical details. As these Colonial Revival houses replaced Craftsman/Bungalows in popularity, interiors changed from dark-stained wood panels and trim to white or pastel-painted woodwork and plaster, and from stairways of straight square lines to curving balusters and round newel posts and spindles.

This revival also included styles from the colonial American Southwest: Spanish Colonial, Mission, and Pueblo (also referred to here as "Aztec") revivals. Like the Mediterranean styles, these had masonry walls, flat or slightly pitched red-tile roofs, round-headed doors and windows, and wrought-iron balconies. Also, stucco exteriors and a low heavy appearance imitated adobe missions and haciendas, and log ends protruding below the parapets (wall-tops) echoed Native American pueblos. Another period feature was an outside patio with low masonry walls. Interiors tended to lack woodwork and to have round-headed doors and windows and heavily textured plaster on the walls.

In contrast to this look to the past, Art Deco and the International Style (Bauhaus) were inspired by the latest achievements of science and technology—automobiles, air travel, radio communication, electricity, and new materials like plastic, celluloid, rayon, and metal alloys. These houses were flat-roofed squares or rectangles with stucco, concrete, or metal walls. They had long bands of windows, including ones around corners. They also had glass-block windows (as well as metal windows, doorframes, and tracery) and rounded corners and streamlined trim. These houses lacked porches and other large exterior projections.

Other changes the decade brought were concrete houses, breezeways (enclosed spaces between houses and garages), awnings, shutters, sunken living rooms, air-conditioning, linoleum floors, walls covered with Masonite and canvas, Celotex (wood-fiber board), knotty-pine boards, plywood exterior and interior coverings, door chimes, fluorescent lighting, colored bathroom fixtures, cabinets under kitchen sinks, all-metal (and all-gas and all-electric) kitchens, faucets that mixed cold and hot water, bathtub alcoves, circuit-breakers instead of fuses, and picket fences.

30

Cleveland's imposing homes
CLEVELAND, OH.

WEST CHESTER, PA.

LIVING ROOM OF ABOVE HOUSE

ENGLISH STYLE

CHATTANOOGA, TN.

IN CONNECTICUT

CAPE COD

CELTIC   LOS ANGELES

MODEL HOME

HOUSTON, TX. (ABOVE)

1930 CHEVROLET

CHARACTERISTIC STUCCO WALLS and FLAT ROOF ON PUEBLO STYLE ("AZTEC")

note VARIOUS TYPES OF WINDOWS ON ILLUSTRATED HOUSES

"CARMEL STONE" CHIMNEY →

TAR-AND-GRAVEL FLAT ROOF

COLOR in Bathroom Fixtures

SOUTHERN STYLE

THE MOSAIC TILE COMPANY 205 Coopermill Road ZANESVILLE, OHIO
NEW YORK · CHICAGO · ST. LOUIS · LOS ANGELES · SAN FRANCISCO

MONTGOMERY WARD & CO

This 5 Room HOUSE **$552** others up to **$1688**

KIT~BUILT

Garages **$92⁰⁰** *up*

ALADDIN MILLS

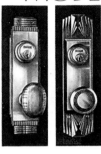

THERMOSTAT

R&E RUSSWIN *RUSSELL C ERWIN* DISTINCTIVE HARDWARE

millions of families gain new leisure with Minneapolis-Honeywell Automatic Heat Control

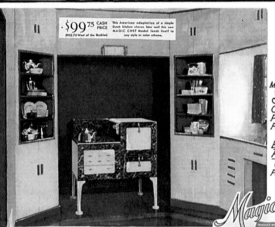

30

MONTGOMERY WARD OFFERS COLORED PLUMBING FIXTURES AT BARGAIN PRICES (SEE PRECEDING PAGE)

$99.75 CASH PRICE ($112.75 West of the Rockies)

This American adaptation of a simple Dutch kitchen shows how well this new MAGIC CHEF Model lends itself to any style or color scheme.

Magic Chef PRODUCT OF AMERICAN STOVE COMPANY

MOSAIC

NEW~ STYLE "TABLETOP" (FLATTOP) STOVE

PATRICIAN · $195 CASH PRICE ($210 West of the Rockies)

Pardee Tiles

NEW!

CHURCH TOILET SEATS AVAILABLE IN MARBLEIZED COLORS!

Royal Tiles . . .

Across the Hellespont came the good looking Alexander in 334 B. C. Triumphantly he entered Susa and Persepolis with the old Persian King, Darius III, on the run. In these cities were the wonderful tile friezes now treasured in the Louvre, . . . amber lions, dusky archers . . . tiles with that wonderful green-blue glaze so characteristic of that period. To please his two new wives, who were Persian princesses, Alexander introduced Western (Grecian) ideas into tiles;—just as Pardee today creates the most modern motifs in tile, without sacrificing the beautiful ancient treatments.

SEARS, ROEBUCK   TUDORS
"PENNSGROVE" MODEL

KIT HOUSES
GORDON~VAN TINE

5 Rooms, Bath .. **$1814**

PEBBLE BEACH, CA.

PASATIEMPO, CA.

"HOMELANDS" SPRINGFIELD, MA.

CALIFORNIA RANCH STYLE DESIGNED BY WM. W. WURSTER, "CREATOR OF THE CALIFORNIA RANCH HOME"

1931 CADILLAC V~16

1931 Chrysler

OLDE ENGLISH RUSTIC

SAN FRANCISCO ROW HOUSE

31

CLAPBOARD BUNGALOW

KITCHEN

KITCHEN

How an expert would light your kitchen

CAPE COD

COLONIAL YELLOW · VERDAS GREEN · GOLDEN YELLOW
APPLE GREEN · IVORY · BLUE
TOBACCO BROWN · CREAM GRAY · GOLDEN BROWN

SWP HOUSE PAINT—Looks and Wears Best. Costs Less by the Job

MINNEAPOLIS~ HONEYWELL new "ELECTRIC CLOCK" MODEL →

THESE NEW THERMOSTATS INTRO. OCT., 1931

ALLIED QUALITY GROUP

SHERWIN-WILLIAMS
PAINTS · VARNISHES · LACQUERS

Tune in Paul Whiteman and the Allied Quality Paint Men over the N. B. C. network every Tuesday at 8 P.M. (Eastern Standard Time)

G.E. (new)

THOUGH WHITE WAS A MOST POPULAR EXTERIOR COLOR, MANY OTHER HUES AVAIL., AS IN THESE COLOR CHARTS.

LETTUCE · ORANGE · SKY BLUE
LAVENDER · YELLOW · ROSE
JADE · CHINESE RED · BLUE

ENAMELOID—The Rapid Drying Decorative Enamel

SWP Trade-Mark Registered
COVER THE EARTH
ATLANTIC · OCEAN
AFRICA · EUROPE

LAUNDRY SINK

GRAY STONE · OAK · SLATE
DUST COLOR · BLUE · WALNUT BROWN
TILE RED · GREEN · MAHOGANY

FLOOR ENAMEL—For Interior Wood and Concrete Floors

KOHLER "SIBLEY" →

31

NEW "Standard" PLUMBING FIXTURES
NEO-CLASSIC

STYLES INTRODUCED

AVAIL. IN 9 COLORS and WHITE

WITH FITTINGS OF HARMONIOUS DESIGN

Standard Sanitary Mfg. Co.
DIVISION OF AMERICAN RADIATOR & STANDARD SANITARY CORPORATION

KOHLER "DOWNING"

KOHLER

NEO-CLASSIC DESIGN; PEMBROKE MODEL,

POPULAR MAGAZINE COVERS OF 1932

House & Garden's
MODEL HOME OF 1932 DISPLAYED IN NEW YORK CITY AT W. + J. SLOANE CO.

LARGE PALLADIAN WINDOW

1932

MEDITERRANEAN

GARAGE AT LEFT

Open House

FLOOR PLAN OF MODEL HOME

BRICK ENGLISH STYLE

WORST YEAR OF THE GREAT DEPRESSION, AND FINAL YEAR FOR MUCH NEW CONSTRUCTION, UNTIL 1936!

SEATTLE

LIVING ROOM OF MODEL HOME

LIVING ROOM OF SEATTLE HOUSE ABOVE

MODERN AMERICAN STUCCO COTTAGE A VERY MODERN DESIGN FOR 1932!

SMALL MEDITERRANEAN

SOUTHERN STYLE

RECREATION ROOM IN ATTIC

TUDOR COTTAGE

NORMAN

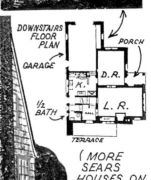

BAY WINDOW UNUSUAL IN THIS ERA! OAKLAND, CA.

the GENERAL ELECTRIC KITCHEN

DREAM KITCHEN COME TRUE

...consult the General Electric Kitchen Institute

"CLIFTON"

"HILLSBORO"
(FACE BRICK)

"LYNNHAVEN"

new QUIET 1-PIECE TYPE

"Standard" PLUMBING FIXTURES

NEW SEARS, ROEBUCK KIT HOUSES FOR 1932

DOWNSTAIRS FLOOR PLAN

PORCH

GARAGE

K.

D.R.

½ BATH

HALL

L.R.

TERRACE

(MORE SEARS HOUSES ON FOLLOWING PAGE)

"BROOKWOOD"

"MAPLEWOOD"

"HAMMOND"

IN SPITE OF THE GREAT DEPRESSION, SEARS INTRODUCED NEARLY **20** OF THESE NEW "HONOR-BILT" HOUSE KIT STYLES IN 1932 !!

"ELLISON"

"TRENTON"

8 ROOMS, 2½ BATHS

"JEFFERSON"

8 ROOMS, 3 BATHS

CAPE COD

"CORNING"
7 ROOMS, 3½ BATHS

"WORCHESTER"
(BRICK)

"GRAFTON"

TRADITIONAL BUNGALOW
(OLD-FASHIONED
DESIGN FOR 1932)

"TORRINGTON"
7 ROOMS
2½ BATHS

184

K
L.R.
BATH HALL CL CL
PORCH

32

OLDSMOBILE
STRESSES VALUE FOR 1932

"RICHMOND"

"ELLSWORTH"

K
D.R.
L.R.
BATH
CLO CLO

SOUTHERN STYLES

CENTRAL HEAT DUCTS

COLONIAL

"NORWICH"

Shop at
SEARS
and Save

"CRESTWOOD"

SEARS BATHROOM FIXTURES (WHITE, GREEN, ORCHID OR IVORY)

HERCULES

SEARS "HERCULES" HEATERS

SEARS
ROEBUCK
KIT HOUSE

PLAN →

KIT,
$1164.

HALF-
TIMBER
TUDOR

PORCH

KEF
DINING
ALCOVE

KITCHEN
12'-0" X 13'-0"

DINING OR
BED ROOM
10'-4" X 11'-0"

BATH
5 X 7

BED ROOM
10'-0" X 13'-0"

HALL

PASSAGE

C L C

BED ROOM
12'-0" X 13'-0"

LIVING RM
15'-0" X 19'-6"

TERRACE
8'-0" X 15'-0"

FLOOR PLAN

33

TUDOR STYLES WITH PLAIN
STUCCO WALLS (W/o HALF TIMBER
TRIM)

DUPLEX →

AWNING ↓

IN APTOS, CA. (4 VIEWS)

CORNER WINDOW NEAR FRONT DOOR

DINING ROOM

HEAVILY TILED BATH (TUB and W.C. ALCOVES)

OAKLAND, CA.

DETACHED
GARAGE
MATCHES
STYLE OF
HOUSE

PACIFIC
GROVE,
CA.

1933 PONTIAC 8

SCENE IN A NEW JERSEY PLUMB. FIXT. FACTORY

33

A VARIETY OF
AVAILABLE
COLORS ←

SEARS
KIT HOUSE

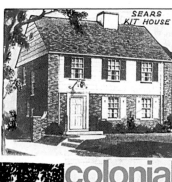

colonial

DAY and NIGHT
WATER
HEATER

1933 DOUBLE HEAT
TRAP (PATENTED)

1933½
PLYMOUTH
DELUXE
COUPE

"We're a Two-car Family
AND THEY'RE
BOTH PLYMOUTHS!"

↗
RUSTIC
STONE and
SHINGLE
EXTERIOR

33

$3,500

SOFT GREEN AND BLACK AND ALUMINUM

ULTRA-MODERN

EARLY "FLAT-TOPS"

CLEVELAND, OH.

PREFABRICATED

BELOW:
ONE OF THE LAST EXAMPLES OF THE PUEBLO/
AZTEC STYLES = RARE VARIATION!

UNFORTUNATELY THIS PACIFIC GROVE HOUSE WAS TORN DOWN.

SPANISH COLONIAL

IN CARMEL, CA.

SAN FRANCISCO

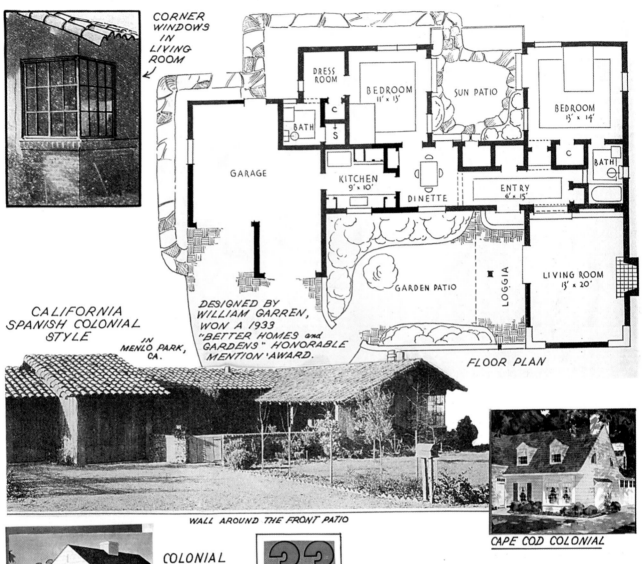

CORNER WINDOWS IN LIVING ROOM

DRESS ROOM

BEDROOM 11' x 13'

SUN PATIO

BEDROOM 13' x 14'

BATH

C
S

GARAGE

KITCHEN 9' x 10'

DINETTE

ENTRY 6' x 15'

C

BATH

GARDEN PATIO

LOGGIA

LIVING ROOM 13' x 20'

CALIFORNIA SPANISH COLONIAL STYLE

IN MENLO PARK, CA.

DESIGNED BY WILLIAM GARREN, WON A 1933 "BETTER HOMES and GARDENS" HONORABLE MENTION AWARD.

FLOOR PLAN

WALL AROUND THE FRONT PATIO

CAPE COD COLONIAL

COLONIAL

A SIMPLIFIED MODERN VARIATION OF 1933

33

"Connecticut Yankee" colonial

IN CONNECTICUT

SALT BOX STYLE

(ASYMMETRICAL GABLE)

FLOOR PLAN

CURTAINS UNDER SINK,
CABINETS AT EITHER
SIDE

KITCHENS

Monel Metal never rusts.

STREAMLINE
SINK ABOVE IS
OF STAINLESS...

MONEL METAL

33

thousands of owners of
Monel Metal sinks, cab-
inet and range tops

TABLE TOPS AND STOVE TOPS ALSO AVAIL.
IN MONEL METAL, AS ABOVE.

LATEST TYPE
OF FLAT~TOP
STOVE WITH
LOW OVEN

MODERN BUILT~IN CABINETS UNDER SINK ↑

FLOOR COVERED IN SEALEX LINOLEUM
PATTERN #7327, "ANDALUSIA," (ABOVE)
"   " 7340, "COURT" →

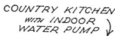

PATTERN
#3240,
"MOSAIC"

WITH FREE~STANDING SINK

COUNTRY KITCHEN
WITH INDOOR
WATER PUMP ↓

COLONIAL

CAPE COD SPLIT~LEVEL HOUSES

Ⓢ = AVAIL. IN KIT FORM FROM SEARS, ROEBUCK

COLONIAL

FRENCH STYLE Ⓢ

WHITEWASHED BRICK WALLS

(2 DUTCH COLONIAL MODELS INTRO. BY SEARS ROEBUCK IN 1934.)

CAPE COD

34

Model Home Sold

ENGLISH / NORMAN COTTAGE STYLE

TACOMA, WA.

ENGLISH TUDOR

STEEL~ SASH

NRA

CASEMENT WINDOWS

WOOD~ SASH

(THIS MODEL INTRO. '33)

SHINGLED TUDOR

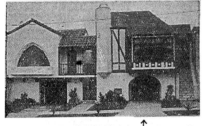

SAN FRANCISCO
ROW
HOUSES

MANY OF
THESE
HAVE A "TUNNEL
ENTRANCE,"
GARAGE AND
BASEMENT AT
STREET
LEVEL.

Detached Patio Home

$6950.

34

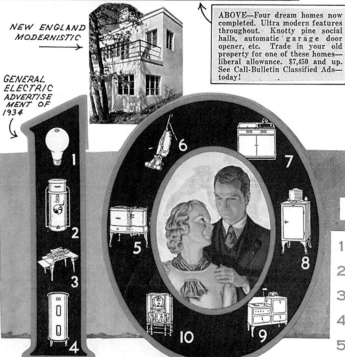

BRAND~
NEW
HOUSES
IN
SAN
FRANCISCO,
ADVERTISED
IN
JUNE,
1934

NEW ENGLAND
MODERNISTIC

GENERAL
ELECTRIC
ADVERTISE
MENT OF
1934

ABOVE—Four dream homes now completed. Ultra modern features throughout. Knotty pine social halls, automatic garage door opener, etc. Trade in your old property for one of these homes— liberal allowance. $7,450 and up. See Call-Bulletin Classified Ads— today!

BUY YOUR HOME NOW

MISSION TERRACE
BRAND NEW PATIO PLAN

Canvas walls throughout, fireplace, radio tower, spacious social hall, equipped bar, cedarized closets, beautiful tile bath with separate stall shower, furnace. Full price $6500.

The Ten Best Home Servants

1	**VISION** MAZDA LAMPS	
2	**COMFORT** OIL FURNACE	
3	**NEATNESS** IRONER	
4	**CONVENIENCE** WATER HEATER	
5	**YOUTH** CLOTHES WASHER	
6	**CLEANLINESS** VACUUM CLEANER	
7	**SANITATION** DISHWASHER	
8	**HEALTH** REFRIGERATOR	
9	**FOOD** RANGE	
10	**ENTERTAINMENT** RADIO	

STONE CONSTRUCTION

CAR :
1934
DODGE

Arkansas Posts sponsored the erection of 103 community center buildings—clubhouses for everybody—in 1934, with the aid of Federal relief labor and funds. Native stone was used in the clubhouses shown on this page. Above, the building at Lincoln, in the Ozarks; below, the hut at Judsonia, in the center of the State

34

COLONIAL

JUDSONIA, ARK.

NATURAL WOOD

MAIN FLOOR PLAN

GROUND FLOOR PLAN

Because the house is built upon a slope both floors are ground floors.

ANGLED FIREPLACE and SINGLE-WALL CONSTRUCTION

1934 FUTURISTIC BEACH HOME IN BRIDGEHAMPTON, LONG ISLAND, N.Y.

DESIGN IS FAR AHEAD OF ITS TIME !!

BOTH LEVELS SHOWN

LANSING C. HOLDEN, ARCHITECT

UPPER LEVEL

CORNER WINDOWS

1934 CALIFORNIA RANCH-STYLE "STUDIO HOME" IS SEVERAL YEARS AHEAD OF ITS TIME!

UNDER CONSTRUCTION

A studio-type California home in Brittany. Double walls, real brick fireplace, stall shower, ample closet space. Close to transportation, schools, theaters, churches and excellent shopping facilities. Advertised in the Classified Ads today.

IT'S HERE---FROM THE
Chicago World's Fair
THE MANUFACTURER'S
CELOTEX EXHIBIT

This is a Celotex Interior

Diagram shows 98 sq. inches extra space

GRAMERCY
THE NEW SHELF-SPACE
KOHLER LAVATORY

WHY NOT arrange for a Lavette—first floor washroom—in your home? Think of the time and steps it will save, the convenience when guests come. Here is a new lavatory built for this need. Note the shelf top and shelf sides, forming flat, wide spaces for the tumblers, toilet articles and extras.

Every detail of the new Gramercy is planned for your convenience. All-metal fittings are placed on the back wall, out of the way. Their chromium finish is quickly and easily cleaned with a damp cloth. The Gramercy is made in one piece, of vitreous china (white or in color).

Distinctive, it is designed to match the quiet, one-piece, hygienic Integra shown in sketch of a Lavette below. Price* of Gramercy is $37.40 and Integra is $45.85.

KOHLER
OF
KOHLER
planned plumbing

NEW

Quiet
TOILET
of graceful lines

...ANOTHER KOHLER MATCHED FIXTURE

HERE is a modern, compact, unobtrusive toilet—the new K of K Bolton Reverse Trap. It has quiet, positive syphonic action, providing a thorough cleansing flush with minimum quantity of water. It absolutely prevents contamination of domestic water supply, since inside bottom of tank is ¾ inch above highest point of bowl rim.

The low tank gives the Bolton exceptionally graceful proportions. Tank and bowl securely held together with four bolts. There are no exposed flush connections. The Bolton stands away from the wall—in many replacement installations tile or plaster need not be torn away—this saving goes a long way toward paying for the fixture.

The new Bolton matches the Metropolitan Bath—modern lines, flat surfaces, beveled corners. $26.64 (subject to change), in white, less delivery, piping, installation.

TYPICAL DINING ROOM

new! CISTERN TANK BOLTS DIRECTLY ONTO THE BOWL, THUS ELIMINATING THE USUAL CONNECTING "ELBOW" PIPE.

HEATING
Air Conditioning

General Motors
DELCO OIL BURNERS

COMBUSTIONEER
Automatic Underfeed
COAL STOKERS

FUTURISTIC BATHROOM

Fitting a space 5' x 7', the new Lavashower embraces in one compact unit a full-sized tub, shower, lavatory and cabinet for linens and accessories. White or colors. Lavashower Corp.

(EXTRA ½-BATH)
"Lavette"

NRA
MEMBER
WE DO OUR PART
34
A GOVERNMENT-BUSINESS CO-OPERATIVE AGENCY, 1933 TO 1935.
U.S.

NEXT-DOOR NEIGHBORS (THESE 2 HOUSES IN PACIFIC GROVE, CALIF.)

SPANISH-MEDITERRANEAN

ENGLISH-NORMAN STYLE, ABOVE (HOUSE BEGUN IN 1934, COMPL. IN 1935.)

CAPE COD

EASTERN

35

COLONIAL STYLES

MONTEREY COLONIAL

SOUTHERN

F.H.A. BEGINS —AND WITH IT, A SLOW BUT STEADY PICK-UP IN THE CON-STRUC-TION OF NEW HOMES AGAIN!

CAR: 1935 CHEVROLET MASTER DELUXE

SPANISH-MEDITERRANEAN (ABOVE)

SPANISH-MEDITERRANEAN

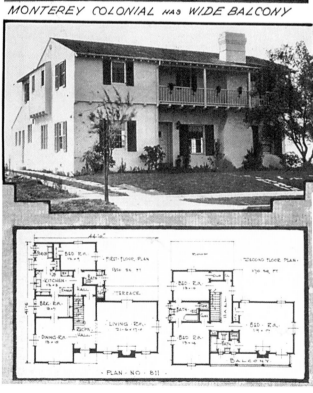

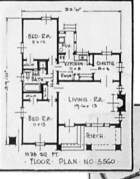

FLOOR · PLAN · NO · 5560

MONTEREY COLONIAL HAS WIDE BALCONY

· PLAN · NO · 811 ·

TYPICAL STAIR HALLS

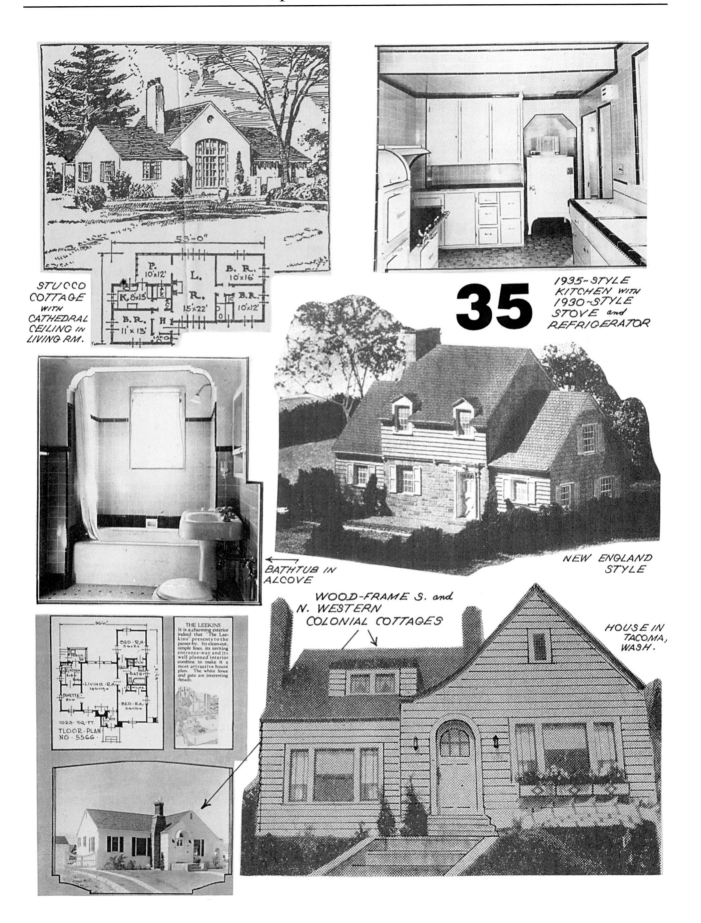

STUCCO COTTAGE WITH CATHEDRAL CEILING IN LIVING RM.

53'-0"

35

1935-STYLE KITCHEN WITH 1930-STYLE STOVE and REFRIGERATOR

BATHTUB IN ALCOVE

NEW ENGLAND STYLE

WOOD-FRAME S. and N. WESTERN COLONIAL COTTAGES

HOUSE IN TACOMA, WASH.

THE LEEKINS
It is a charming exterior indeed that "The Leekins" presents to the passer-by. Its clean-cut, simple lines, its inviting entrance-way and its well planned interior combine to make it a most attractive house plan. The white fence and gate are interesting details.

1023 SQ. FT.
FLOOR PLAN NO. 5566

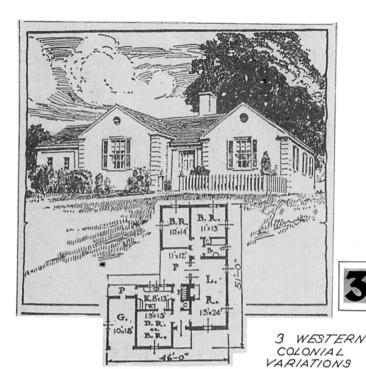

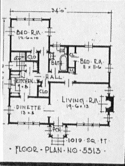

35

3 WESTERN COLONIAL VARIATIONS

CAPE COD (BELOW)

$750.00 F.O.B

KIT-BUILT HOUSES

Cabin

AVAIL. 1932 TO 1937, ONE OF SEARS ROEBUCKS' LATER KIT-BUILT HOUSES: THE 1935 "STRATHMORE" AT $1584. → (SEARS' EX~ "HONOR-BILT" KIT HOUSE DEPT. CLOSED IN 1940.)

$1,350.00 F.O.B.

CAR: 1935 WILLYS "77"

KIT-BUILT HOUSES

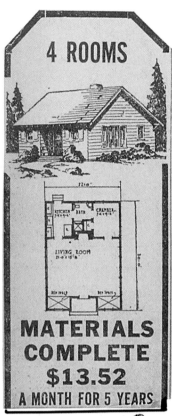

4 ROOMS

MATERIALS COMPLETE
$13.52
A MONTH FOR 5 YEARS

4 Room Colonial Cottage
WITH BATH AND SHOWER

Materials Complete
$19.63
A Month for 5 Years
Wiring and Plumbing Excepted

A PLEASANT small home, easily and economically constructed and suitable for any small family. Efficient and convenient, this home offers 4 large rooms and a bath. A delightfully charming exterior is equaled by its snug and lovely interior arrangement and finish. Cash price for our materials, $942.58.

35 The day we invented the spinet!

The year was 1935. Family fun centered around the radio and the piano. But smaller houses of the day called for smaller pianos. Small, but with a big sound.

So Winter invented the spinet.

MATERIALS COMPLETE
$19.67
A MONTH FOR 5 YEARS

"BESTILE"
FIBREBOARD ARTIFICIAL TILE AVAIL.

THE STORY OF "BESTILE"

"BESTILE" is a wall tile manufactured in sheet form on a patented water-proof, pressed fibreboard, with a porcelain-like, glazed surface.

This beautiful, sanitary wall tile, available to home-builders at a substantial saving over ordinary tile, has been used in many hundreds of homes in every section of the country.

Furnished in a complete range of colors with cap, base, and all necessary "Trim" to harmonize with the color scheme.

35

EARLY USE OF FLUORESCENT TUBE LIGHTING (RIGHT, and BELOW)

MODERN MIXING FAUCETS ON THIS COMPACT KOHLER BATHROOM SINK

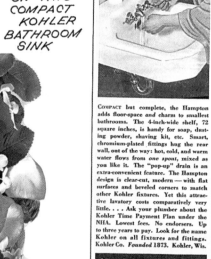

KOHLER HAMPTON

COMPACT but complete, the Hampton adds floor-space *and* charm to smallest bathrooms. The 4-inch-wide shelf, 72 square inches, is handy for soap, dusting powder, shaving kit, etc. Smart, chromium-plated fittings hug the rear wall, out of the way: hot, cold, and warm water flows from *one* spout, mixed as you like it. The "pop-up" drain is an extra-convenient feature. The Hampton design is clear-cut, modern — with flat surfaces and beveled corners to match other Kohler fixtures. Yet this attractive lavatory costs comparatively very little. . . . Ask your plumber about the Kohler Time Payment Plan under the NHA. Lowest fees. No endorsers. Up to three years to pay. Look for the name Kohler on all fixtures and fittings. Kohler Co. *Founded 1873.* Kohler, Wis.

KOHLER OF KOHLER

Left, Diagram of Tube Lamp Installation for Direct and Indirect Lighting; Upper Right, Ornamental Units Used as Mirror Lights in Boudoir; Lower Right, Theater Lighting, with Closeup of Lamp

BATHS

See Sensationally New **"Standard"** PLUMBING FIXTURES at San Diego Exposition

STANDARD'S LUXURY "NEO-ANGLE BATH" TUB FITS IN *A SQUARE SPACE WITH TUB AREA SET DIAGONALLY.*

(ONE OF THESE TUBS ABOARD A STREAMLINED S.P. TRAIN OF 1938, OF ALL PLACES!)

35

Neo-Angle Bath designed for all ages. It provides every bathing facility in the one fixture. The corner pattern is shown below.

The Neo-Angle bath with its new safety, convenience and more ample bathing space, all resulting from its two integral seats. The Neo-Line Sink, a beautiful design of flowing curves, is furnished with a marvelously efficient cabinet having revolving shelves. See other fixtures that are also exclusive in design and features. All are available on "Standard" Time Payment Plan.

Standard Sanitary Mfg. Co.
GENERAL OFFICES, PITTSBURGH, PA.
Division of AMERICAN RADIATOR & STANDARD SANITARY CORP.

"Standard" PACIFIC Plumbing Fixtures are made at Richmond, California.

A MODERN BATHROOM of 1935

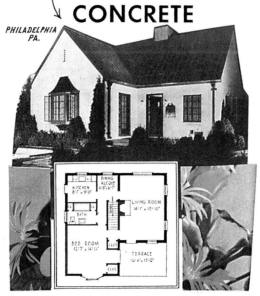

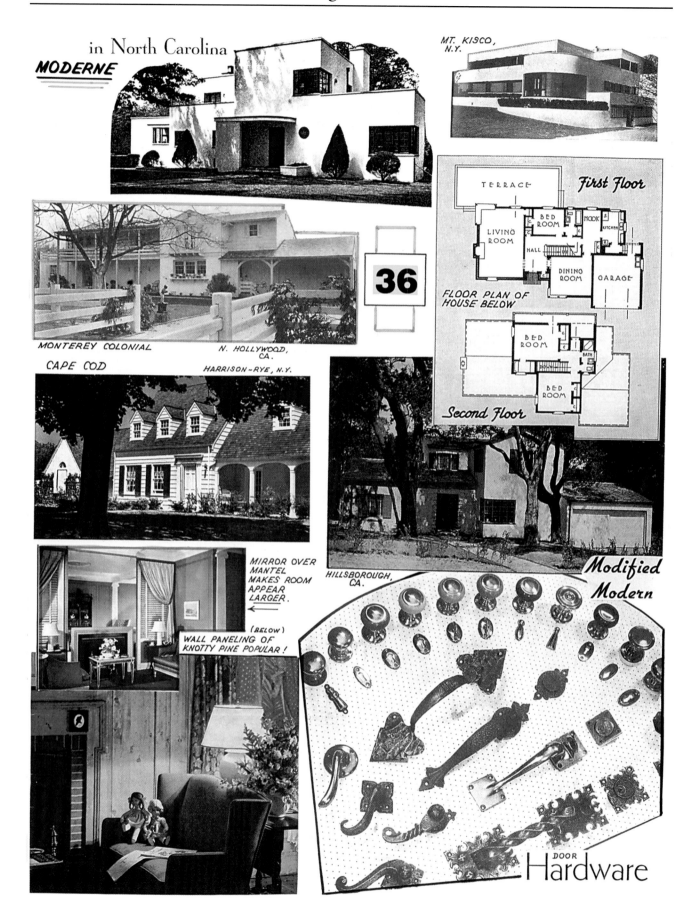

in North Carolina

MODERNE

MT. KISCO, N.Y.

First Floor

TERRACE

LIVING ROOM

BED ROOM

NOOK

KITCHEN

HALL

DINING ROOM

GARAGE

FLOOR PLAN OF HOUSE BELOW

36

BED ROOM

BATH

BED ROOM

Second Floor

MONTEREY COLONIAL

N. HOLLYWOOD, CA.

CAPE COD

HARRISON-RYE, N.Y.

MIRROR OVER MANTEL MAKES ROOM APPEAR LARGER.

(BELOW)

WALL PANELING OF KNOTTY PINE POPULAR!

HILLSBOROUGH, CA.

Modified Modern

DOOR Hardware

SUNBEAM AIR CONDITIONING

AIR CONDITIONING STILL UNCOMMON IN 1936.

A tuck-away kitchen, just right for the summer cottage or basement playroom

Announcing
THE KITCHEN SINK THAT SCIENCE BUILT

THE CRANE
Sunnyday
36 CABINET SINK

These attractive new solid aluminum or bronze
KAWNEER WINDOWS-

NEVER NEED PAINTING!
ALWAYS OPERATE EASILY!
ARE WEATHER-TIGHT...
QUICKLY INSTALLED..

BRIGGS

NOW— N-83 *Beautyware* COLOR COMBINATIONS!

CRANE

"Now we have a beautiful bathroom— everything Kohler quality"

Modern Necessity
KOHLER DENTAL LAVATORY

New convenience and cleanliness

KOHLER OF KOHLER
PLANNED PLUMBING AND HEATING

FOOT BATHING
BATH AND SEAT IN ONE PIECE
SOAKING
SHOWERING

a new tub!

STOKOL
FOR CONTROLLED HOME HEAT

CENTRAL HEAT

PORCELAIN DOUBLE LAUNDRY SINK (CRANE) MOST LAUNDRY SINKS MADE OF GRAY CONCRETE.

FAUCETS

KITCHEN and BATH FIXTURES

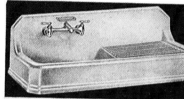

Single Drainboard Sink—42 or 52-Inch

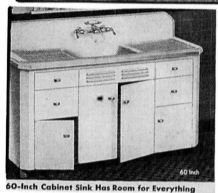

Medicine Cabinets

36

CLAWFOOT TUBS:
TRADITIONAL
AND
MODERNIZED
TYPES
ARE
BOTH
AVAIL.

60-Inch Cabinet Sink Has Room for Everything

Lowest Priced $14.50 Tub Only
Tub, With Legs

Round Front $5.45 Lavatory Only
Lavatory—Only

Syphon Wash- $12.50 Less Seat
down Closet

Built-In $31.25 Tub Only
Recess Tub

Roomy Lavatory $6.95 Lav. Only
Colonial Design

Reverse Trap $14.50
Closet—Quiet

Attractive Unit Closet $21.95 Without Seat
Quick Acting — Quiet

Vanity Top $20.45 21x24
Lavatory

Built-In Tub $37
Modern Design

WARDS LAUNDRY TUB

Cast Iron Tray
Made in the West
$10.25

ONE-PIECE LEAK-PROOF LA
$7.65
Smooth—Leak-Proof—
Seamless

New Low Tub $22.95 Tub Only
5 Feet Long

A Really Smart $9.95
Lavatory—Only

Syphon Wash-
down Closet
$13.95

All Wards Sinks, Closets,
Lavatories, and Tubs are made
in the West by Western Workmen

SPLIT~LEVEL

LOS ANGELES

SAN MATEO, CA.

MENLO PARK, CA.

1937 NASH~LAFAYETTE

1937 PACKARD "120"

KITCHEN 10'-6"×11'-0"
RANGE
BREAKFAST NOOK 5'-6"×11'-0"
DINING-ROOM 11'-0"×13'-6"
BEDROOM 8'-6"×10'-0"
DEN 9'-0"×10'-0"
GARAGE 10'-0"×16'-0"
LIVING-ROOM 12'-6"×23'-0"
SEAT

FIRST FLOOR

SECOND FLOOR

BEDROOM 11'-0"×16'-0"
HALL
BATH 6'-0"×6'-6"
BEDROOM 12'-0"×14'-3"
STORAGE 10'-0"×16'-0"
BEDROOM 12'-6"×17'-6"
STORAGE 12'-6"×16'-6"

ENGLISH STYLE

Kelvin Home

DESIGNED BY KELVINATOR, TO SHOWCASE ITS HOME APPLIANCES

(A CHILDHOOD HOME OF THE AUTHOR)

BERKELEY, CA.

37

BRICK~WORK, CORNER WINDOWS AND PICKET FENCES POPULAR

IN CONCRETE MASONRY

MARBLEHEAD, MA.

FLOOR PLAN

SPLIT~LEVEL

SAN MATEO, CA.

HOUSING PROJECT, LIBERTY SQUARE, MIAMI, FLORIDA

CAPE COD

ULTRA~ MODERN

MAUMEE, OH.

CLEVELAND, OH.

ART DECO

VIRGINIAN STYLE

PARTIAL ~ STONE COLONIAL

Evergreen Park's First.

WESTPORT, L.I., N.Y. (ABOVE)

CAPE COD

MODERN ~ STYLE "BAY WINDOW"

GARAGE ~ DOOR WINDOWS OUT OF STYLE AFTER 1937.

37

THERMOSTATS

AUTOMATIC CONTROLS MH

BUILD Your HOME

WORLD'S LOWEST PRICED QUALITY HOME $495 AND UP

ALADDIN KIT ~ BLT. COTTAGE

HUMIDITY CONTROL

CHRONOTHERM

Minneapolis-Honeywell

DA-NITE ACRATHERM

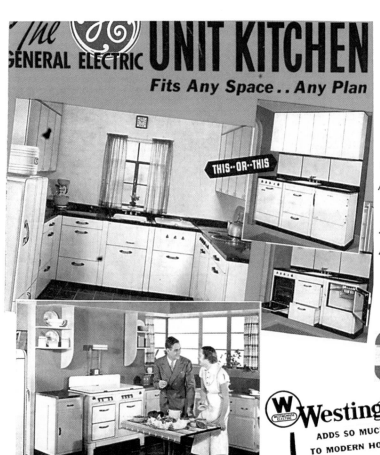

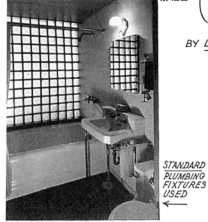

DUTCH COLONIAL REVIVAL (RARE BY 1938)

Home is full of happiness, the one place you love best— May it always mean for you ease and pleasant rest

CAPE COD House at Bartlesville, Oklahoma

WASHINGTON, D. C.

CAPE COD STYLES HIGHLY POPULAR!

HACKENSACK, N. J.

38 white houses

DENVER, CO.

SAN FRANCISCO MODERNE

FORMAL STYLE

DETROIT, MI.

NEW ENGLAND STYLE (OR CAPE COD)

STONE FACADE DOWNSTAIRS

CHICAGO

THESE 3 KIT HOUSES JOINED THE SEARS, ROEBUCK LINE IN 1938.

BONDEX...The World's Standard Waterproof Cement Paint

SOUTHERN

KIT HOUSES

MODERN URBAN STYLE

MODERN HOMES at mill prices

The VICTOR—4 Rooms and Bath (Materials) $1025

Save $300 AND UP

TRADITIONAL

Gordon-Van Tine Co.
World's Largest Specialists in Home Building Since 1865

BUILT IN 30 DAYS

PRECISION-BUILT Homes

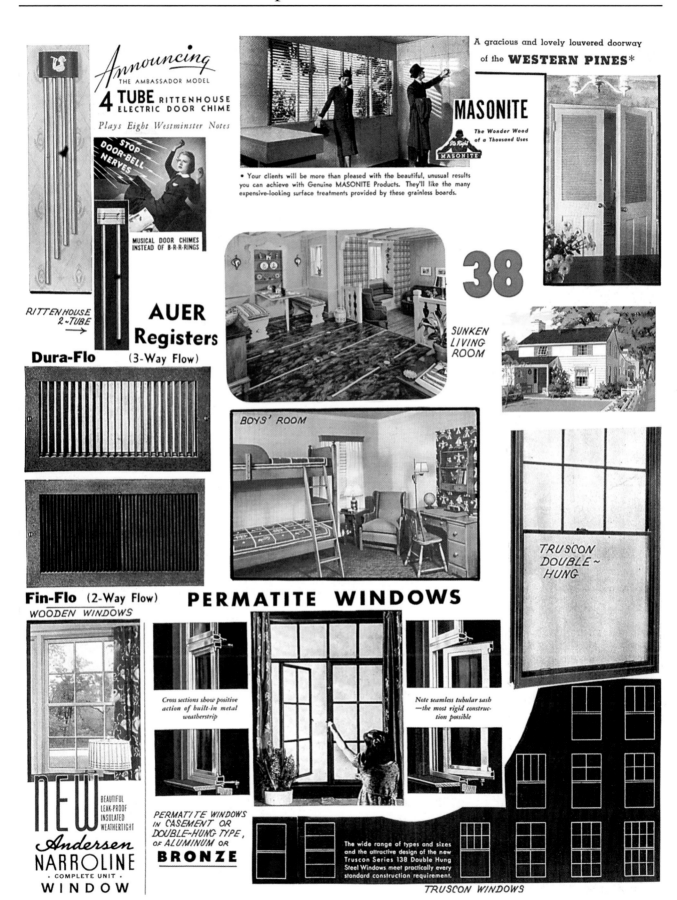

Announcing
THE AMBASSADOR MODEL

4 TUBE RITTENHOUSE ELECTRIC DOOR CHIME

Plays Eight Westminster Notes

STOP DOOR-BELL NERVES

MUSICAL DOOR CHIMES INSTEAD OF B-R-R-RINGS

RITTENHOUSE 2~TUBE →

Dura-Flo

AUER Registers
(3-Way Flow)

Fin-Flo (2-Way Flow)

A gracious and lovely louvered doorway of the **WESTERN PINES***

MASONITE
The Wonder Wood of a Thousand Uses
It's Right MASONITE

• Your clients will be more than pleased with the beautiful, unusual results you can achieve with Genuine MASONITE Products. They'll like the many expensive-looking surface treatments provided by these grainless boards.

38

SUNKEN LIVING ROOM

BOYS' ROOM

TRUSCON DOUBLE~ HUNG

WOODEN WINDOWS

PERMATITE WINDOWS

Cross sections show positive action of built-in metal weatherstrip

Note seamless tubular sash —the most rigid construction possible

neW
BEAUTIFUL LEAK-PROOF INSULATED WEATHERTIGHT

Andersen
NARROLINE
• COMPLETE UNIT •
WINDOW

PERMATITE WINDOWS IN CASEMENT OR DOUBLE~HUNG TYPE, OF ALUMINUM OR **BRONZE**

The wide range of types and sizes and the attractive design of the new Truscon Series 138 Double Hung Steel Windows meet practically every standard construction requirement.

TRUSCON WINDOWS

MINNEAPOLIS-HONEYWELL *Control Systems*

BROWN INDUSTRIAL INSTRUMENTS
NATIONAL PNEUMATIC CONTROLS
MINNEAPOLIS-HONEYWELL REGULATOR
COMPANY...MINNEAPOLIS, MINNESOTA

Look for the "M-H" Symbol. It is your assurance of lasting, carefree heating comfort.

"ACRATHERM" THERMOSTAT

ANNOUNCING THE NEW MONEL "DUOCRAT"

38 *the Sink and the Range Are One*

Monel Sink and Magic Chef Range in one Beautiful, Step-Saving Unit...

CENTRAL HEAT

SO YOU GOT A HOLLAND TOO!— BET YOU'RE SAVING PLENTY ON COAL!

RIGHT!— LESS WORK, LESS COAL, MORE COMFORT!

HOLLAND FURNACE COMPANY
HOLLAND, MICHIGAN

World's Largest Installers of Home Heating and Air Conditioning Systems

KITCHEN

1866 **CURTIS WOODWORK**

CORNING

"HALLSTADT" CEILING LIGHT FIXTURE GLOBE, 1 OF 4 DESIGNS

As little as '4.00 WEEKLY Buys a Completely Equipped *Hotpoint* **ELECTRIC KITCHEN**

Hotpoint Electric Kitchens— for Modest Homes

VICTOR *In-Bilt* **KITCHEN VENTILATORS**

BEAUTY in BLUE...

Suntile

RUUD GAS WATER HEATERS FITTED WITH TANKS OF MONEL

'MONEL' is a registered trademark applied to an alloy containing approximately two-thirds nickel and one-third copper.

20 YEAR GUARANTEE

RUUD MANUFACTURING COMPANY

NEW FLAT-BOTTOM, LOW-SIDED BATHTUBS AVAILABLE FROM CRANE, AS WELL AS KOHLER.

BATHROOM

FROM MID-1930s TO EARLY 1960s, STANDARD'S BIGGEST SELLING W.C.s ARE THE WASHDOWN, VERTICAL-FRONT "MODERNUS" (EVOLVING FROM FORMER "EJECTO,") and THE NEW REVERSE-TRAP "CADET." NAMES NOT ALWAYS DISPLAYED ON THE UNITS, HOWEVER.

CRANE FIXTURES

KOHLER FIXTURES

with *Color Balanced* **Suntile**

BALBOA IS., CAL.

MEMPHIS, TN.

GEORGIAN   MODIFIED FOR THE SOUTHWEST

DALLAS, TX.

STUCCO EXTERIORS

CHICAGO, ILL.

BURBANK, CALIFORNIA

BRICK HOUSE W. HIP ROOF

BIRMINGHAM, ALA.

NEW ALBANY, IN.

KINGSPORT, TENN.

SHINGLED EXTERIOR

SIMPLE BOX COTTAGE

LOW COST HOUSING
IN VARIOUS REGIONS OF U.S.A.

DELRAY BEACH, FLORIDA   THE MACKLE CO., BUILDER
(WITH EARLY TYPE OF CARPORT)

HEMPSTEAD, L.I., N.Y.

NORFOLK, VA.

39

BREEZEWAY CONNECTS TO GARAGE

CAPE COD VARIATIONS
(WITH AND WITHOUT DORMER WINDOWS)

UP

BEDRM   BEDRM   BEDRM

$3,772 in Oreland, Pa.

BEDROOM ABOVE ATTACHED GARAGE

GARAGE   KITCHEN
DINING RM   LIVING RM
DOWN

WITH REVERSE FLOOR PLAN OF HOUSE ABOVE

CL   CL
BED ROOM 10'-0"x14'-6"   BATH   KITCHEN 8'-0"x9'-6"
BED ROOM 10'-0"x13'-0"   DINING ROOM 10'-0"x12'-0"   GARAGE 8'-6"x14'-0"
LIVING ROOM 13'-0"x15'-0"   PORCH
CL   CL

ORELAND, PA.

Columbus, Ohio

JACKSON, MISS.

MIAMI, FLORIDA

CEDAR RAPIDS, IOWA

TERRACE

BED ROOM
12'-0"x12'-0"

KITCHEN
8'-0"x 8'-6"

BATH

LIN

CL

CL

DINING
7'-6"x 8'-6"

GARAGE
10'-0"x 20'-0"

LIVING ROOM
14'-0"x 17'-0"

MIDLAND, MICH.

$3,000 including lot

Courtesy, Concrete Products Inc.

LOW COST
ARIZONA
HOUSES

TUCSON, AZ.

HOUSES IN VICTORVILLE, CALIF.

VARIATION: Plan reversed; Flat Roof

MODERNE

39

SCREEN
SLEEPING PORCH

TUXEDO PARK, N.Y.

BLT.
1938 to 1939

**BUILT
for
$1950**
★ using

This is LOW-COST HOUSING at its best —
materials of unquestioned quality, economically installed, without waste of lumber or labor and *sure to*
stand up under the wear and tear of a lifetime.

WELDWOOD is phenolic-resin bonded — withstands
any degree of summer heat or winter cold — any
amount of rain, sleet or snow.

WELDBORD is hot-pressed for high moisture resis-
tance — made with cross-grain faces for extra
rigidity — free from grain-raise, checking or patches
— takes paint, enamel or stain perfectly — wallpaper may be applied directly to its surface.

UNITED STATES PLYWOOD CORPORATION
World's Largest Producers and Distributors of Plywood

WELDWOOD
FOR SIDING
and
WELDBORD
RESIN-BONDED *Hardwood Plywood* WALLBOARD
FOR INTERIOR WALLS
AND CEILING

★ FIR, PINE
and
HARDWOODS

GAMBREL
ROOF

TRI-
DORMERED
CAPE CODS

BOTH ILLUSTR.
FEATURED 1939
IN "DUTCH BOY
PAINT ADS.

1939
LINCOLN ZEPHYR

Treat Your HOME Like An OLD FRIEND

"DUTCH BOY"

A House that is LOVED

TACOMA, WA.

FLOOR PLAN OF ABOVE HOUSE

ENTRY HALL
KITCHEN
BATH
BEDROOM
DINING ALCOVE
HALL
CLOS.
BEDROOM
ENTRY HALL
CLOS.
LIVING ROOM

39

LAFAYETTE, LA.

Home of Ralph Seymour, Darien, Conn. Concrete foundation, walls and floors. Architect: Fred J. Wallis, Westport, Conn.

Concrete home of Maurice Heymann, Lafayette, La. Architects: N. W. Overstreet and A. H. Town of Baton Rouge, La., and Jackson, Miss.

Cottage or Mansion
CONCRETE gives your new home beauty, comfort and safety...*at low annual cost*

BOISE, ID.

REAR VIEW

You are invited to visit us at our home at the Golden Gate Exposition.

SEATTLE

TREASURE ISLAND, CA.

YEARS BEFORE THE "ASBESTOS SCARE"

On the sidewalls of this House...

Beauty that never grows old!

...the architect specified J-M "Shake" Textured Asbestos Shingles... fireproof, durable, and weather-resistant...

Not until you actually touch these Johns-Manville Asbestos Shingles, do you realize they are not made of wood. That's how faithfully they reproduce the charm and texture of old, hand-split "shakes"!

Johns-Manville has recaptured this traditional beauty in a modern material . . . asbestos-cement. By the very nature of this composition, J-M Asbestos Shingles cannot burn or rot, and they require no paint to preserve their lasting charm. Throughout the years, their virtual freedom from maintenance will prove an important factor in minimizing upkeep on this house.

The charm of New England and of the **WESTERN PINES***

. . . in this delightful Cape Cod Cottage designed by Royal Barry Wills, Architect. This gracious little home shows the millions visiting the colorful Golden Gate Exposition how the Western Pines enhance the simple dignity of our traditional architecture. Inside the cottage, the Western Pines impart authentic character, friendly charm and beauty to every room.

REAR

FRONT

*Idaho White Pine   *Ponderosa Pine   *Sugar Pine

— THESE ARE THE WESTERN PINES —

HOUSE IN PHOENIX, ARIZONA

Johns-Manville
JM

Nofuze Multi-Breakers for homes

PATRICIAN

BOR-IN
39

MONK'S CORNERS, S.C.

3½ GAL. W.C. IS YEARS AHEAD OF ITS TIME!

MIRRORED WALLS   SEA ISLAND, GA.

MARLITE WALLS
bathroom

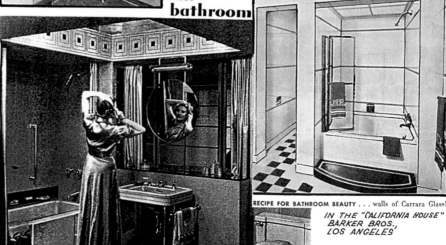

RECIPE FOR BATHROOM BEAUTY . . . walls of Carrara Glass!

IN THE "CALIFORNIA HOUSE"
BARKER BROS.,
LOS ANGELES'

CRANE FIXTURES

Chapter
7

1940-1949

Building materials were in short supply in this decade because of the war effort, so housing construction declined sharply, especially in the first two years of the war. After that, prefabricated, modular, and mobile housing became the successor to the kit houses of the 1920s and '30s and made construction faster and cheaper. After the war was over, war bonds purchased during the war could be redeemed with interest to pay for new houses when building materials became more plentiful.

For the most part, architectural styles during the 1940s were not new but rather continuations and variations on styles from the previous two decades. Most houses were colonials (Cape Cod, Federal, and Georgian) with asymmetrical gables and windows, or with bays or porticos added, to distinguish them. But some were new versions of Art Deco and International Style and were labeled "Ultra-Moderne" and "Futuristic."

After the war, the tract- and prefabricated-housing industries came into their own to provide housing for millions of returning servicemen. Tract houses made up planned neighborhoods of similar houses and culminated in Levittowns, built in New York in the 1940s and '50s. Most of these houses were smaller than those of the previous decade. A finite amount of building materials had to be spread as far as possible, and veterans, even with government assistance, did not have much money to spend. So most houses were four- or five-room, one- or one-and-a-half-story frame houses with a one-car garage or carport. Some were expandable houses, built to be readily enlarged as family finances improved. Most were gabled, with a faint hint or two of a traditional style.

The "ranch-style" house grew in popularity during this decade. It was long and low, with several small windows, and one larger one (a "picture window") for the living room.

New also during the 1940s were aluminum siding, garbage disposals, automatic dishwashers, overhead garage-doors, chrome tubular-legged furniture, and steel-panel exterior walls. Reappearing were log houses, wallpaper, exposed-beam open ("cathedral") ceilings, wood interior paneling, clerestory and octagonal windows, and cedar-shake siding.

MODERN HOMES

7 rooms and 3 baths, with provision for future room and bath over 2-car garage. On a high knoll of a full acre, with extensive views. Price $22,800.

IN N.Y. STATE

JUST COMPLETED AT LAWRENCE FARMS

Plank Siding

STUCCO

RIVERSIDE, CT.

IVORY-COLORED PLASTIC SWITCH PLATES and PLUG RECEPTACLE PLATES

40

CEDAR SHINGLE SIDING

LIVING ROOM

FLOOR PLAN NO 5017

POPULARLY PRICED AMERICAN HOME KIT
Economical to Build

ENTRY

with Carey LONG-LIFE PRODUCTS

Designed by architect Edgar W. Archer of Louisville, Kentucky, this house typifies American efficiency. Convenient and practical in every detail, yet hospitable and attractive, inside and out. Five generous-sized rooms, compactly built to limit cost and save steps. Upstairs space for two extra rooms when needed.

Built with CAREY Products, this house is distinguished by low maintenance cost. The colorful, Cork-Insulated Shingle roof is stormproof. Exterior walls of lifetime Careystone Siding, lend a note of modern beauty; minimize maintenance. CAREY Rock Wool Insulation assures maximum comfort, winter and summer; pays back its cost in fuel savings.

This home, No. 107, may be built under liberal F.H.A. plan and paid for in easy monthly installments. Mail coupon today for folder and directions for securing blue-prints of this and other distinctive homes.

THE PHILIP CAREY COMPANY
Dependable Products Since 1873
LOCKLAND, CINCINNATI, OHIO

Look for this ASQU label on the roofing you buy—it is your assurance of longer roof life—lower roof cost per year.

SOUTHERN COLONIAL   "PRECISION-BUILT" HOME
READY FOR OCCUPANCY IN 30 DAYS

NEW HOME OF NORMAN TAUROG, M-G-M, director of "Broadway Melody of 1940" and "Young Tom Edison." Designed by Rollin Pierson.

WEST COAST

IN TAUROG MANSION

PACIFIC GROVE, CA.

SEATTLE

A NEW and better Chronotherm at a price everyone can afford . . . Styled by Henry Dreyfuss the 1940 Chronotherm with Numeral Clock gives you new beauty and new features, including an accurate, easily read numeral electric clock.

DRESSING ROOM, TAUROG MANSION

The New 1940

(Available about March 15th)

CHRONOTHERM

MINNEAPOLIS-HONEYWELL

$29.

8 22

10 50 60 70 80 90

DESIGNED BY HENRY DREYFUSS

ONLY $18 MORE THAN A MANUAL THERMOSTAT
(Installation Extra)

A Product of MINNEAPOLIS-HONEYWELL

Controls and Control Systems for Heating, Ventilating, Air Conditioning, Industrial Processing

Since 1885

KITCHENS

40

TODAY TWICE AS MUCH at ½ PRICE

ICE COLD LEMONADE

BATHS

STANDARD FIXTURES

What a Jewel . . .

IT'S ELJER EQUIPPED, OF COURSE

ALL-BLACK PLUMBING FIXTURES RARE, BUT AVAILABLE SINCE LATE 1920s.

A "½-BATHROOM" DOES NOT INCLUDE A BATHTUB.

A CRANE HALF-BATHROOM

MINNEAPOLIS ~
HONEYWELL
THERMOSTAT

CALIFORNIA
RANCH STYLE
(WIDE,
COVERED FRONT
PORCH TYPICAL
OF MANY)

1941 FORD

CUTLER·HAMMER
MULTI-BREAKER
C·H

WHY
BOTHER WITH
BLOWN FUSES?

Install the new and marvelous convenience of the modern Cutler-Hammer
Multi-Breaker. Then when service fails,
you simply step to the kitchen wall, reset
a little lever that has snapped out of posi-
tion . . . and, presto! your service is completely restored.

convenient and modern

CALIFORNIA
COLONIALS

41

TRADITIONAL
STYLES
PREDOMINATE

WEST COAST STYLE MODERN BUNGALOW
(WITH COLONIAL OVERTONES)

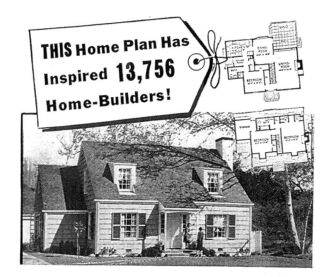

THIS Home Plan Has Inspired 13,756 Home-Builders!

ONE of 178 Popular Home Plans in the 1941 edition of NEW IDEAS FOR BUILDING YOUR HOME

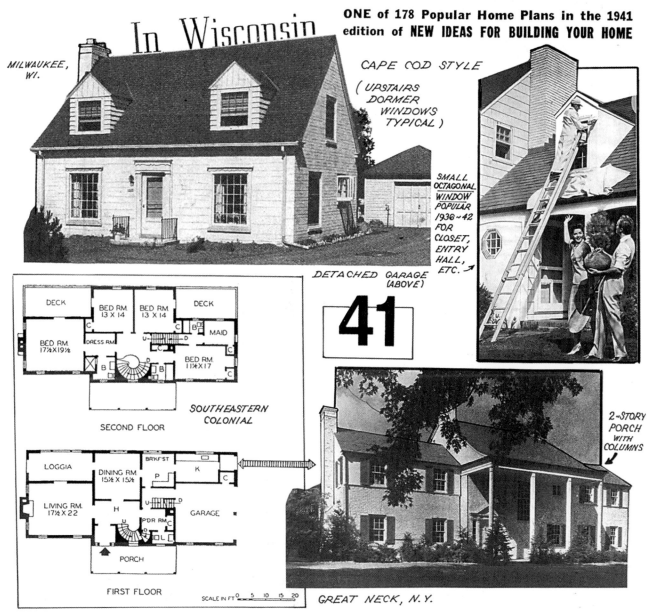

In Wisconsin

MILWAUKEE, WI.

CAPE COD STYLE

(UPSTAIRS DORMER WINDOWS TYPICAL)

SMALL OCTAGONAL WINDOW POPULAR 1936~42 FOR CLOSET, ENTRY HALL, ETC. ➘

DETACHED GARAGE (ABOVE)

41

SECOND FLOOR

DECK | BED RM. 13 X 14 | BED RM. 13 X 14 | DECK

BED RM. 17½ X 19½ | DRESS RM | MAID

BED RM. 11½ X 17

SOUTHEASTERN COLONIAL

FIRST FLOOR

LOGGIA | DINING RM. 15½ X 15½ | BRKFST | K

LIVING RM. 17½ X 22 | H | GARAGE

P'DR RM.

PORCH

SCALE IN FT 0 5 10 15 20

2~STORY PORCH WITH COLUMNS ↙

GREAT NECK, N.Y.

1941 DESOTO

ULTRA ~ MODERNE

41

(ABOVE) CARLTON, OR. HOME OF THOMAS MITCHELL, MOVIE STAR (ENGLISH COTSWOLD STYLE)

BRICK COLONIAL (DALLAS, TX.)

CONCRETE CONTEMPORARY   MILWAUKEE, WI.

MILWAUKEE'S LARGEST CONCRETE HOME (AS OF 1941)

CLOSER DETAIL OF ENTRY and FACADE

3 KIT-BUILT HOUSES (BELOW)

LOW-COST EFFICIENCY HOME

BASEMENT PLAYROOM and 1/2 BATH

AMERICAN HEATING EQUIPMENT

COST NO MORE THAN OTHERS

"*Standard*" PLUMBING FIXTURES

BUILT TO LAST A LIFETIME...

WITH *Carey* LOW UPKEEP MATERIALS

41

A PERFECT POWDER ROOM that features the smart, space-saving "Standard" Marburg Lavatory and Compact Closet.

Architect Paul V. Matkin accomplished something new and important to millions when he designed this smart, two-bedroom home having the efficiency of a modern apartment. Complete with attached garage, utility room, automatic gas heat, hardwood floors. Yet its ownership is within the means of a family having an income of $100 to $125 a month.

PAGE AND HILL CO.

1076 Plymouth Bldg., Minneapolis, Minn.
772 Hudson Terminal, New York, N.Y.

LOG HOUSE

Your HODGSON HOUSE is ready

MODERN KITCHENS

GLASS~BLOCK WINDOW

AMERICAN HEATING EQUIPMENT

↑ BUILT~IN DINETTE

MUELLER *Gas Furnace*

...with Coppes **NAPANEE** cabinets

Coal

Oil

KNOTTY~PINE WALLS

This Sink and Cabinet BY **CRANE**

41

G.E. REFRIGERATOR ↑

OLDER~STYLE KITCHEN LIKE MID~1930s TYPES ↓

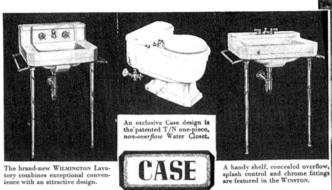

An exclusive Case design is the patented T/N one-piece, non-overflow Water Closet.

The brand-new WILMINGTON Lavatory combines exceptional convenience with an attractive design.

CASE

A handy shelf, concealed overflow, splash control and chrome fittings are featured in the WINSTON.

DISTINCTIVE PLUMBING FIXTURES

CRANE FIXTURES (ABOVE)

SEE **ELJER'S** MODERN DESIGN AND COLOR-STYLING...

NEW FOR '41

MUELLER "STREAMLINE" COLORED TENITE PLASTIC SHOWER HEAD

41 NOTE DIP IN SIDE OF TUB FOR EASY ENTRY and EXIT.

TUB / SHOWER HANDLE

KOHLER of KOHLER

EST. 1873

This modern bathroom has a Kohler matched set—Cosmopolitan "bench bath" with full-size space inside and new Triton mixer (only one handle to turn), Gramercy lavatory with handy ledge and towel bars, and efficient Integra.

See for yourself! The new Times Square bath is smart, practical —meets the needs of all, young or old. It combines with other Kohler pieces to make neat matched sets. (Shown here—Jamestown lavatory; Placid closet.) Look over the complete line—many styles and sizes—

DECEMBER 1941 = U.S.A. ENTERS INTO WORLD WAR 2.

CAPE COD

BECAUSE OF THE W.W. 2 EMERGENCY, VERY LITTLE CIVILIAN HOME CONSTRUCTION DURING 1943.

KENILWORTH, IL.

42 -43

COMBINED

DUTCH ROOF

HACKENSACK, N.J.

"ISLAND KITCHEN" (EARLY EXAMPLE)

BUILT~IN

CORNER FIREPLACE

BRICK HOUSES

ENTRY WAY

WHITE BRICK

SALT LAKE CITY, UT.

FROM MISSOURI!

CLERESTORY UPPER WINDOWS

WINDOW STYLES

FEB., 1942: NEW CAR PROD. STOPS FOR WAR.

FRAME CONSTR.

LADUE VILLAGE, MO.

1942 OLDSMOBILE ("BLACKOUT" MODEL)

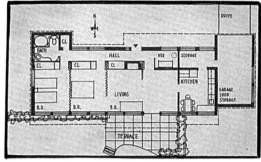

BUY UNITED STATES WAR
SAVINGS BONDS AND STAMPS

A HOME FOR EVERY FAMILY
is the aim of post-war planning

FUTURISTIC

FRENCH MODERN

42 **43**

CHILD'S CLOSET
WITH RAISED FLOOR

Better Living's Ahead FOR ALL AMERICA...

. . in "MIRACLE HOMES" that today's
War Bonds will buy Tomorrow!

Living quarters face south for sun, with windows and doors largely of glass. Wide overhang is so designed as to admit sun's more direct rays (winter, spring, autumn) for heating, help reduce fuel bills to minimum. Deflects rays of summer sun into ground. Miracle interior opens into huge living room, or separates easily into living, dining and extra sleeping space. Streamlined built-in furniture brings new comfort, utility, cleaning ease.

"Miracle Home" by Architect George Fred Keck

MINNEAPOLIS ~
·HONEYWELL CONTROLS

ACHIEVEMENT
Minneapolis and
·Honeywell
the Army-Navy "E"

ARMY
E
NAVY

the Chronotherm
THE NEW CLOCK
THERMOSTAT THAT
SAVES FUEL

Automatic Heating and M-H Controls will be considered for priority rating ... See your heating dealer now!

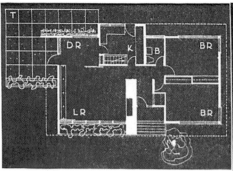

THESE TOP 3 ILLUSTRATIONS ARE INTERIOR DETAILS OF HOUSE ON LOWER RT. CORNER OF PRECEDING PAGE.

PROJECTION TELEVISION IN LIVING ROOM! (VERY FEW HAD T.V. IN '43!!)

PREFABRICATED KITCHEN UNITS PREDICTED

STORAGE
OVEN
PRESSURE COOKER
TOASTER
BOILER
STOVE
COFFEE
CONTROLS
STORAGE

ICE CUBES
QUICK FREEZE
REFRIGERATOR
DISH WASHER
SINK
WORK SHELF

42
□
43

FLATTOP MODERN

livable

CREATE NEW ROOMS

future | built now | future

fut. sto. | future car shelter | work space | future childrens' rooms

living | b. r. 1 | b. r. 2

Plan showing how this house may be enlarged in **two** directions, according to future needs and finances.
(NOTICE UNUSUAL AISLE BATH, w/o TUB)

SEATTLE, WA.

MID~1942 WARTIME PLUMBING FIXTURES (BELOW)

INSULATE TO SAVE VITAL FUEL

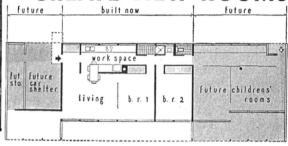

KOHLER of KOHLER

DUPLEXES

NEW FOUR-PIECE POTOMAC SET—*POTOMAC* 5-foot cast iron recess wing bath, enameled inside — with low sides, wide rim and flat bottom, anti-siphon mixer fitting ... *DELTON* 18 x 15-inch enameled cast iron shelf lavatory with 1½-gallon basin, two soap dishes ... Close-coupled, vitreous china *TRYLON* with TriKo seat (not shown) ... *PARKCHESTER* 42 x 22-inch cast iron combination sink (right, below), 8-inch-deep basin for dishes and 13-inch-deep tub for laundry—mixer fitting with swing spout—lustrous, acid resisting enamel.

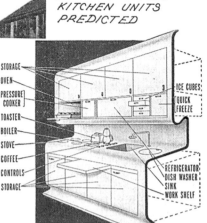

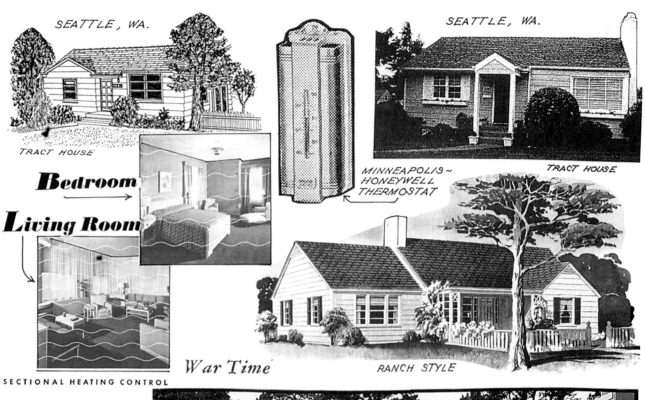

SEATTLE, WA.

TRACT HOUSE

SEATTLE, WA.

TRACT HOUSE

Bedroom →

Living Room ↓

MINNEAPOLIS~ HONEYWELL THERMOSTAT

RANCH STYLE

SECTIONAL HEATING CONTROL

War Time

BING CROSBY'S HOME

2 VIEWS OF BING'S HOME IN PEBBLE BEACH, CA. BUILT TO <u>REPLACE</u> THE CROSBY HOME IN SO. CALIF. WHICH HAD A BAD FIRE IN 12-43.

44

EARLY PREFABRICATED MOBILE/ MODULAR UNITS HELPED TO MEET THE W.W. 2 HOUSING SHORTAGE.

PACIFIC GROVE, CA.

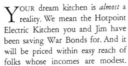

So MANY of us are sick of our old-fashioned kitchen—tired of the bathroom with its noisy closet, high tub and slow-draining lavatory. We want a new bathroom and kitchen—done in the modern style with the latest conveniences—efficient plumbing—bright cheery colors and lots of storage space.

You dream kitchen is *almost* a reality. We mean the Hotpoint Electric Kitchen you and Jim have been saving War Bonds for. And it will be priced within easy reach of folks whose incomes are modest.

← CRANE KITCHEN

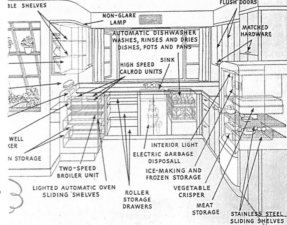

BLE SHELVES

NON-GLARE LAMP

FLUSH DOORS

MATCHED HARDWARE

AUTOMATIC DISHWASHER WASHES, RINSES AND DRIES DISHES, POTS AND PANS

HIGH SPEED CALROD UNITS

SINK

WELL KER

N STORAGE

TWO-SPEED BROILER UNIT

LIGHTED AUTOMATIC OVEN SLIDING SHELVES

INTERIOR LIGHT
ELECTRIC GARBAGE DISPOSALL
ICE-MAKING AND FROZEN STORAGE

ROLLER STORAGE DRAWERS

VEGETABLE CRISPER

MEAT STORAGE

STAINLESS STEEL SLIDING SHELVES

— Buy MORE War Bonds!

FOR YOUR DREAM HOME

44

BATHS

KITCHEN DETAILS

IN SPITE OF THESE 1944 ADVERTISEMENTS, COLORED PLUMBING FIXTURES HARD TO OBTAIN DURING W.W. 2 MATERIAL SHORTAGE.

NATION-WIDE SERVICE THROUGH BRANCHES, WHOLESALERS, PLUMBING AND HEATING CONTRACTORS

CRANE

PLUMBING · HEATING · PIPE · FITTINGS · VALVES

FLATTOP CONTEMPORARY

1945 CONSTRUCTION SLOWED BECAUSE OF LIMITED SUPPLY OF BUILDING MATERIALS.

RANCH STYLES and TRACT HOUSES PREDOMINATE IN EARLY POSTWAR YEARS

45 WAR ENDS

KOHLER SINK

INTERIOR LIGHT

ICE-MAKING AND FROZEN STORAGE

MEAT STORAGE

TWO VEGETABLE CRISPERS

STAINLESS STEEL SLIDING SHELVES

NON-GLARE LAMP

AUTOMATIC OVEN TIMER AND CLOCK

HIGH SPEED CALROD UNITS

TWO-SPEED BROILER UNIT

DEEP-WELL COOKER

AUTOMATIC DISHWASHER WASHES, RINSES AND DRIES DISHES, POTS AND PANS

ELECTRIC GARBAGE DISPOSALL

SINK

LIGHTED AUTOMATIC OVEN SLIDING SHELVES

CAPE COD

PAN STORAGE

HOTPOINT KITCHEN

HOME BUILDERS

Back at last to his old swimming hole!

AMERICAN~STD. TUB

COLONIAL

NUTONE
TRADE MARK
DOOR CHIMES

COLONIAL CHIME

DUTCH COLONIAL REVIVAL

SKYLINE CHIME

MONTEREY, CA. ECONOMY COTTAGE

CONTINENTAL CHIME

2 RINGS FOR FRONT DOOR, 1 FOR BACK DOOR

"JACKKNIFE" SWING-OUT TABLE

CAPE COD   SEATTLE, WA.

46 new CARS PRODUCED AGAIN, BUT HARD TO GET!

Spin the shelves!
Swing the table!

BIG new "SLINKY" SPRING TOY FAD IN 1946!

KITCHENS

ARMSTRONG'S LINOLEUM

New! Exciting! Different!... General Electric lamp research makes cool, soft fluorescent "run around in circles"

It's the new
G-E CIRCLINE LAMP

INTRO. 1946

HOTPOINT

Houses

Pennsylvania

VIRGINIA

CONTEMPORARY

SEATTLE

COLONIAL

RANCH

CAPE COD

REYNOLDS LIFETIME ALUMINUM BUILDING PRODUCTS USED IN THIS CONSTRUCTION

WITH ALUMINUM SIDING

Southern

47

MASTER BEDROOM

DAY & NIGHT

CIRCULAR DRIVEWAY

WESTERN (BELOW)

HIP ROOF

WALLPAPER, MAPLE FURNITURE

TODAY-HEAT TRAP FLUE (PATENTED)

Cedar Shake Walls

IT'S SMART TO BUILD WITH

WEST COAST WOODS

Douglas Fir • West Coast Hemlock • Western Red Cedar • Sitka Spruce

SPECIFY CEDAR SHAKES

Honeywell CLOCK THERMOSTATS are here again!

POSTWAR MATERIAL SHORTAGE EASES UP IN 1947.

Honeywell MINNEAPOLIS CONTROL SYSTEMS

← CRANE THERMOSTAT

Pictures show how General Electric Disposall* shreds food waste, flushes it down kitchen drain. (MORE VIEWS BELOW)

Enjoy the cheerful warm glow of your open fireplace

plus four times more heat and warm air circulation to all parts of the room and even into adjoining rooms

WITH

HEATFORM

THE SUPERIOR HEAT CIRCULATING FIREPLACE

Crane Compac Radiator

STEAM AND HOT WATER HEAT IS STILL AVAILABLE.

with Crane-Line controls.

GENERAL ⓖ ELECTRIC

DISPOSALL

ATTACHED BELOW KITCHEN SINK

47

AMERICAN-STANDARD FIXTURES ←

WOOD-PANELED BATHROOM →

Crane

Replace Old Faucets with *Dial-Ese*

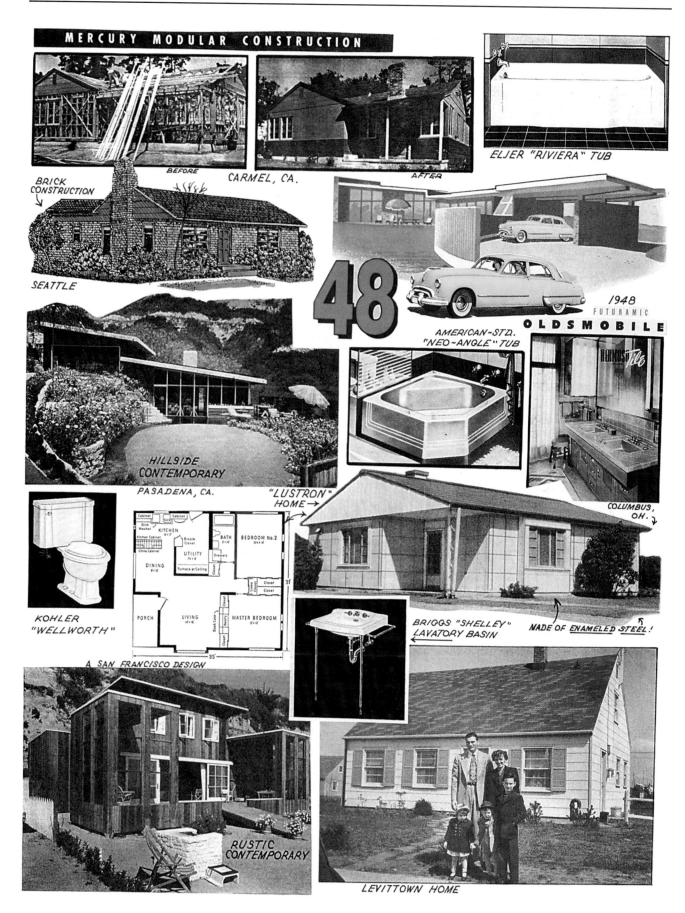

MERCURY MODULAR CONSTRUCTION

BEFORE

CARMEL, CA.

AFTER

ELJER "RIVIERA" TUB

BRICK CONSTRUCTION

SEATTLE

48

1948 FUTURAMIC OLDSMOBILE

AMERICAN-STD. "NEO~ANGLE" TUB

HERMOSA Tile

HILLSIDE CONTEMPORARY

PASADENA, CA.

"LUSTRON" HOME →

COLUMBUS, OH.

KOHLER "WELLWORTH"

A SAN FRANCISCO DESIGN

BRIGGS "SHELLEY" LAVATORY BASIN

MADE OF ENAMELED STEEL!

RUSTIC CONTEMPORARY

LEVITTOWN HOME

EICHLER-BUILT

FROM 1949 TO 1967, MORE THAN 10,000 ULTRA-MODERN EICHLER HOMES WERE BUILT IN CALIFORNIA. (3 VIEWS)

INDOOR/OUTDOOR ATRIUM →

KAISER-BUILT HOMES (BELOW)

OPEN-BEAM CEILINGS

49

1949 KAISER CAR

BACK PATIO

KAISER HOME FRONT ENTRY

SPACE-EFFICIENT KAISER KITCHEN

SHOWER HEAD ALSO FILLS TUB

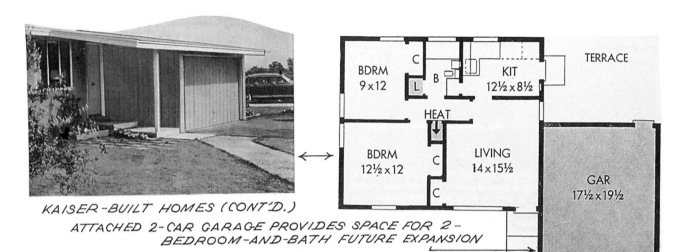

KAISER-BUILT HOMES (CONT'D.)
ATTACHED 2-CAR GARAGE PROVIDES SPACE FOR 2-
BEDROOM-AND-BATH FUTURE EXPANSION

INTERIOR OF MASS-PRODUCED TRACT HOME
IN LEVITTOWN, N.Y. SPACIOUS ATTIC
ALLOWS FOR FUTURE EXPANSION.

SAN FRANCISCO

KIT HOUSES

20,000 RETAIL LUMBER DEALERS
WILL FEATURE THIS HOME IN 1949

PREFABRICATED HOME
CONSTRUCTION

(7 OTHER NATIONAL MODELS
AVAILABLE IN 1949)

NOTE
CORNER
WINDOWS

RANCH-
STYLE
TRACT
HOUSES

CONTEMPORARY

Flat-topped, two-bedroom

BY 1949, MOST HOUSES HAD A
1-CAR ATTACHED
GARAGE.

1949 DE SOTO

Wyandotte
WINTER AIR CONDITIONER

AMERICAN-Standard
First in heating...first in plumbing

"EMPIRE
GAS
BOILER"

HEATER

Open Daily
FOR INSPECTION AT
885 MAPLE ST. — Pacific Grove
10 A.M. to 6 P.M.

.... like to live in a Honeymoon home like this? -
- - - Pacific Grove's first Post Adobe house - - just
completed with all these attractive features ....

* Well-to-wall broadloom carpet throughout
* Clay tile kitchen floor
* Large out-door patio
* Especially-made doors throughout
* Large detached garage
* Artistic landscaping & fencing

* Exceptionally large level lot · · · · 50 by 237 feet
* New Radiant Glass heat
* A large raised hearth fire place
* Tile Pullman Bath
* Thermador built-in cooking unit
* Built-in brick barbeque in kitchen
* Hand-painted designs in kitchen

PHIL D. HASKINS
671   Mermaid — Pacific Grove

HUGH COMSTOCK, NOTED CARMEL, CALIF. BUILDER,
WAS INSTRUMENTAL IN POPULARIZING POST-ADOBES.

KOHLER FIXTURES

A SINK "Just right for your kitchen"
FROM THE COMPLETE CRANE LINE

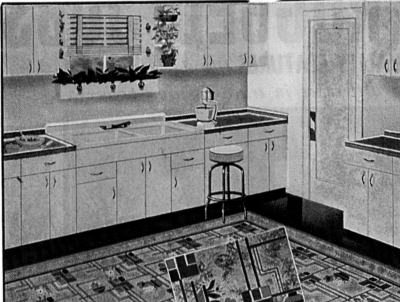

KITCHEN

NATIONAL HOME LIVING ROOM

49

● Two to four comfortable bedrooms ● Spacious living rooms, efficient kitchens, adequate closet and storage space ● With or without basements, garages, porches and breezeways ● Construction includes steel columns and girders, open-web steel beams, insulated exterior walls and ceilings, hardwood floors, aluminum double-hung windows ● No unforseen extras!

First in heating...first in plumbing

AMERICAN-STANDARD KITCHEN SINK ←

National Production Methods *Provide Better Homes for More Families at Less Cost!*

PRESENT PRICES $6,000 AND UP

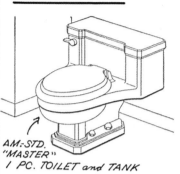

"MASTER" TOILET, "NEO-ANGLE" TUB, "ROXBURY" SINK (ABOVE)

BATHROOMS

AM.-STD. "MASTER" 1 PC. TOILET and TANK

49

ANOTHER BEAUTIFUL BATHROOM BY BRIGGS

Only Briggs makes this Safety-Bottom—the world's safest, most modern bathtub feature!

BRIGGS TUB has BOTTOM w. SAFETY RIDGES.

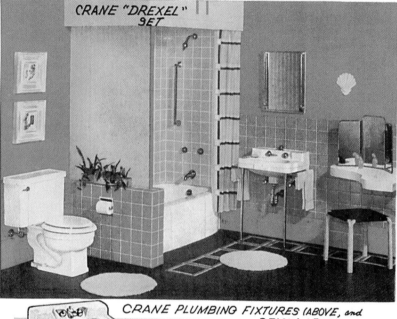

CRANE "DREXEL" SET

CRANE PLUMBING FIXTURES (ABOVE, and BELOW, LEFT)

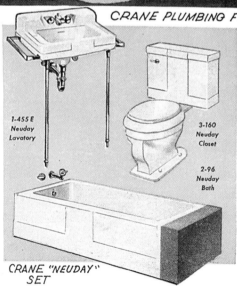

1-455 E Neuday Lavatory

3-160 Neuday Closet

2-96 Neuday Bath

CRANE "NEUDAY" SET

ELJER

MAKERS OF FINE PLUMBING FIXTURES SINCE 1904

ELJER TOILET TANK has INTEGRAL CERAMIC OVERFLOW PIPE (1) and OUTLET VALVE SEAT (2) TO PREVENT RUST

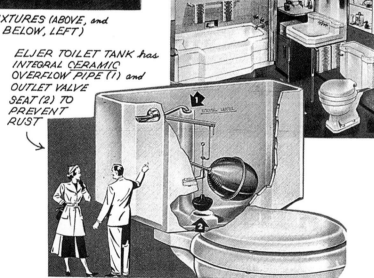

Chapter

8 1950-1959

In this decade, few new styles were introduced. As the United States was recovering from World War II, the resulting prefabricated and tract houses showed less variety of style than the houses introduced in the 1920s and '30s. Most 1950s houses were variations on only a few of the styles of the previous twenty or thirty years—colonial, Cape Cod, ranch, and "modernistic" (also referred to here as "contemporary").

Most of those were watered-down versions of the originals, or watered-down versions of the already altered and simplified variations on the eighteenth and nineteenth century originals. What was called a Cape Cod, for example, was any house with a high-gabled roof, usually with dormers, and with the front door in the side. But now the Cape Cod is outfitted with a breezeway, a garage, and a screened-in side porch. The ranch style is almost any long low house. A Southern Colonial is a two-story gabled house with front columns. A "modernistic" house is a square with a flat roof and horizontal brickwork trim. And a "chalet style" is a high-gabled house with some extra vertical boards on the gable face, but no other details of a Swiss or Tudor building. Only one style, referred to here as "contemporary," differs much from all the others. Generally, it has a flat roof and many windows. It often has two stories, and it appears to have elements of the International and Prairie styles.

Most houses of the 1950s were small and had one or, at most, one and a half stories. They contained no more than six or seven rooms. Many were still prefabricated, so many that one construction company advertised in 1954, "Aladdin houses are not prefabricated," though, ironically, Aladdin was a major manufacturer of kit houses in earlier decades. Tract houses were also available; Levittowns were still being built and sold as late as 1957.

Mostly, the 1950s was a decade of technological innovations and of increasing luxuries for houses as the nation became more prosperous. Television, for example, was becoming so common that even Levittown houses had built-in TV sets by 1950. Other new items were side-facing garages, folding interior doors, partial room dividers, telephone jacks in walls, sliding glass patio doors, indirect lighting, two-bathroom houses, crank-out windows (either vertical or horizontal), thermopane windows, bathroom sinks in vanity cabinets, and Tappan electronic ovens (precursors to microwave ovens).

CITY OF PARIS EXHIBIT HOME

"NORMANDIE" CAROLANDS, CA.

DE LUXE SUBDIVISION HOMES

RANCH STYLE

SIDEWAY-FACING GARAGE A NEW IDEA! ↓

BUILT-IN 12" TV (LEVITTOWN) →

DISTINCTIVE HOMES in CRESCENT PARK
$22,000 to $30,000.

SOUTHERN COLONIAL

WEST VIRGINIA

TRACT STYLE HOUSE (TRADITIONAL)

LEVITTOWN

IN W. VA.

50

America's Top-Value Station Wagon...

1950

Jeep

LEVITT ADDS 1950 MODEL TO HIS LINE
New house has carport, tile bath and a television set—for $7,990

new BEIGE FIXTURES INSTEAD OF FORMER WHITE, IN 1950 LEVITTOWN HOUSES

If you make $45-$50 a week you can own a "Thrift Home"

60 DIFFERENT MODELS!

National HOMES

Presenting the NEW 1950 National Homes "Thrift Home"
LOWEST-COST QUALITY HOME ON THE MARKET!

THIS 5 ROOM **ALADDIN** READI-CUT HOUSE $1492 FREIGHT PAID
Slightly higher west of Missouri River

HOW TO BEAT THE HIGH COST OF BUILDING

Experts Call It "The Easiest Home to Build Yourself"

AT LAST!
A Home You'll Be Proud to Own
COMPLETE FOR LESS THAN
$3650⁰⁰

PHONE PLUG-IN JACKS ADD MOBILITY

KNOTTY PINE PANELING STILL POPULAR

LATER KNOWN AS "CURTITIONS"

50 LARGE EXPANSES OF GLASS IN SOME LIVING ROOMS

← PARTIAL ROOM DIVIDERS A NEW VOGUE →

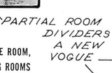

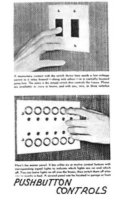

KITCHEN EQUIPMENT

VIKON TILE CORPORATION, Dept. S3, Washington, N. J.

Whatever your plans may be, a new home, or remodeling of your present one, investigate the advantages of featherlight steel, aluminum and stainless steel Vikon Tiles—for use on both walls and ceilings.

COLOR FUSED ON METAL

"Original Individual Metal Tile" Established 1926

CROSLEY ALL-STEEL KITCHEN

MALARKEY PLYWOOD CABINETS

VIKON METAL TILES

Case

Fine Vitreous China advanced design makes good homes better

LID AND PAN RACK

CHOPPING BLOCK

SHARP KNIFE DRAWER

RECESSED HANDY SHELVES

SNACK BAR

RECIPE FILE

SILVER DRAWER

SLIDING TOWEL BAR

OVERSIZE UTENSIL STORAGE

TRAY RACK

LINEN AND PLACE MAT DRAWERS

REVOLVING CORNER SHELVES

SWING OUT SUGAR AND FLOUR BINS

SLIDING SOAP & CLEANSER RACK

METAL-LINED BREAD AND CAKE DRAWERS

Sixteen step-and-bend saving ideas embodied in this modern kitchen built with Malarkey plywood.

"MARCIA" LAVATORY SINK

BATHROOM FIXTURES
"CRITERION" LAVATORY SINK

CRANE
the preferred plumbing

CRANE
the preferred plumbing

LOWER IN 1950 = BOWL 14" HI
It's the New
Case ONE-PIECE

CRANE FIXTURES AVAIL. IN 8 COLORS OR WHITE

"DIANA" LAVATORY SINK

VIKON
VIKON METAL TILE

Universal-Rundle

LAVATORIES—Available in both vitreous china and enameled cast iron. Sizes vary from the 18 x 14-1/2 inch "Cinderella" to the 27 x 20 inch "Chateau." Chrome leg, china pedestal, counter and wall-hung models to fit every need.

BATHTUBS—Rigid cast iron bodies are made in three styles: corner, recess and leg models. The recess tub is either 4-1/2 or 5 feet in length and designed with a wide rim that makes a spacious seat. All tubs have U-R special multi-coat vitreous enamel finish.

FITTINGS—The new, exclusively designed line of Luxury-Trim chrome-brass fittings is made of the very finest materials, styled to conform to the classic lines of the fixtures. Strictly a quality line, yet it carries a popular price tag.

WATER CLOSETS — Both styles, either close-coupled or wall-hung types, are available in many patterns. Choice of three flushing actions may be had. All units are of Hi-Fired Vitreous China.

SINKS—Single and double drainboard cabinet sinks and combination cabinet sinks and laundry trays with acid-resisting enamel tops. Also, single and double compartment

AMERICAN-OLEAN TILE

"STERLING" (KIT)
RANCH STYLE

CHOICE OF 57 DESIGNS

INTERNATIONAL MILL AND TIMBER CO.
DEPT. C. 121   BAY CITY, MICHIGAN

TRADITIONAL

"EARLY AMERICAN" MAPLE FURNITURE IN STYLE

LUXURY BEDROOM SUITE

NEW!

OLDSMOBILE "HOLIDAY" SEDAN

"GALLERY"~STYLE LIVING ROOM

INDOOR / OUTDOOR LIVING ROOM WITH INDIRECT LIGHTING

51

G.E. ELECTRIC KITCHEN

CAPE COD

CONTEMPORARY HOMES

PASADENA, CA.

BRIGGS FIXTURES

CASE SINK

SKY BLUE

Cadillac

1952 CADILLAC

PACIFIC GROVE, CA.

All you want in your dream kitchen IS HERE!
Youngstown Kitchens

NATIONAL HOME

3-Bedroom Ranch-Type *$8,995* UP →

SLEEPING ← LOFT

"A~FRAME"

CLERESTORY WINDOWS IN LIVING ROOM

MINNEAPOLIS~ **Honeywell** *THERMOSTATS*

POPULAR IN THE 1950s

Virtue BROTHERS OF CALIFORNIA CHROME DINETTES

Expandable **MALARKEY HOUSE**

MALARKEY BRAND PLYWOOD USED

BATH
BED-DEN ← 2ND STAGE
BEDROOM
DRESSING
LIVING BEDROOM
BATH
TERRACE
KITCHEN
CARPORT
1ST STAGE →

CHALET STYLE →

BACKGROUND FOR MODERN LIVING
Hermosa Tile REAL CLAY

52

ALL ILLUSTRATED FIXTURES BY UNIVERSAL-RUNDLE.

Whitest! Yes, U-R Arctic White fixtures are *whiter by actual scientific test* than any other bathroom fixtures made. That means extra beauty, extra sparkle!

Quiet performance and smart, one-piece styling make this new, space-saving Como ideal for installations where unobtrusive flushing action is desired.

American-Standard bathroom

CRANE

CRANE

BRIGGS

ELJER

THIS CRANE BATHROOM CAN BE REMODELED TO CREATE 2 !

two bathrooms – a must in every modern home!

Bathroom Fixtures

PEDESTAL URINAL IS *PRACTICAL*, BUT SELDOM USED IN PRIVATE HOMES.

53

BELOW: U/R CLOSET BOWL HAS UNUSUALLY LARGE SQUARE TRAP-WAY.

KOHLER "COSMOPOLITAN" TUB and "GRAMERCY" SINK IN "CERULEAN BLUE"

BELOW, LEFT: UNIVERSAL/RUNDLE LAVATORY SINK IN "AZURE BLUE."

ur

ur

KOHLER

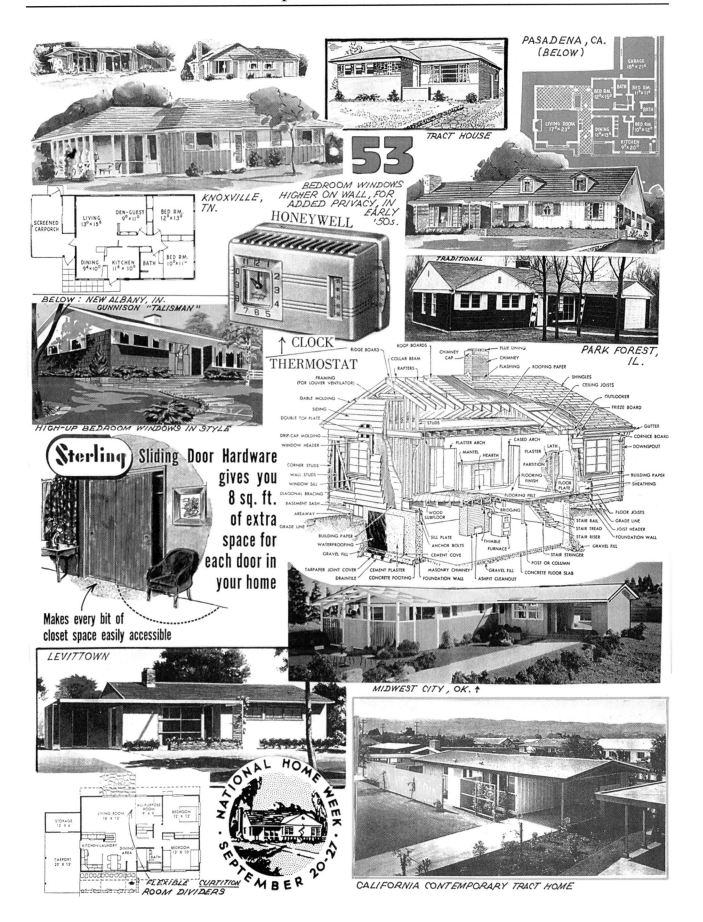

PASADENA, CA.
(BELOW)

GARAGE
18⁶ x 21⁶

TRACT HOUSE

53

KNOXVILLE,
TN.

BEDROOM WINDOWS
HIGHER ON WALL, FOR
ADDED PRIVACY, IN
EARLY '50s.

HONEYWELL

↑ CLOCK
THERMOSTAT

TRADITIONAL

PARK FOREST,
IL.

BELOW: NEW ALBANY, IN.
GUNNISON "TALISMAN"

HIGH-UP BEDROOM WINDOWS IN STYLE

Sterling Sliding Door Hardware
gives you
8 sq. ft.
of extra
space for
each door in
your home

Makes every bit of
closet space easily accessible

LEVITTOWN

MIDWEST CITY, OK. ↑

NATIONAL HOME WEEK • SEPTEMBER 20-27

FLEXIBLE CURTAIN
ROOM DIVIDERS

CALIFORNIA CONTEMPORARY TRACT HOME

FABRICATED HOME

"SPLIT~LEVEL"

KIT~BLT. HOUSES

You can build a PEASE Home yourself ...and save!

Build a Ready-Cut

Ranch - type home, 64 feet wide, with three bedrooms

$5350

1953 CHEVROLET

$3128

Designs As Low As $2608

"LIBERTY" HOMES

Save 30% *to* 40%

Don't pay several hundred dollars more than necessary when you build a home! Buy direct from our mill at our low, factory, freight-paid price. We ship you the lumber cut-to-fit, ready to erect. Paint, glass, hardware, nails, etc., all included in the price. Plans furnished—also complete building instructions. No wonder our customers write us that we saved them 30% to 40%. Architecturally approved construction. (Not prefabricated.)

ABOVE CORNER WINDOW BY *Thermopane*

LOF GLASS

Bow Windows

Double-Hung Windows

U/R Food Waste Disposer! Revolutionary new "Undercut" action makes this the most *quiet* disposer!

53

KITCHENS

FORMAL DINING ROOMS LOSING FAVOR TO LARGE "EAT~IN" KITCHENS.

USED BRICK and ISLAND COUNTERS

CONTINUED POPULARITY of RANCH STYLE

1-STORY WITH BASEMENT

ROOM OPENS TO PATIO

54

SIMPLICITY IN MANY INTERIOR DESIGNS

Eichler HOMES

NO DEALERS' OR AGENTS' PROFITS IN ALADDIN PRICES—BUY DIRECT!

GOOD HOUSES NEVER GROW OLD— ALADDIN HOUSES ARE NOT PREFABRICATED

EICHLER CONTEMPORARY (CALIFORNIA)

DUPLEX (POST~ADOBE CONSTRUCTION ON LOWER FLOOR)

ALADDIN 5-ROOM HOUSE

BUILD YOUR OWN HOME

$1995 FREIGHT PAID

Slightly Higher West of Missouri River

"Best Sellers" BY PAGEMASTER KIT HOUSES

EXCITING NEW HOME DESIGNS FOR 1954!

Pagemaster HOMES

$3,490.00

THE FREMONT—24'x32'—2-bedroom beauty —lots of living at minimum cost.

$4,736.00

THE DEAN—1194 sq. ft.—including garage, 3 bedrooms, compact kitchen, large closets.

$5,224.00

THE KAYE—1146 sq. ft.—4 large bedrooms, U-shaped kitchen, sheltered entrance, hip roof— Deluxe throughout.

THE ALDRIDGE—1100 sq. ft. including garage—2 bedrooms—features economical floor plan, large rooms, low modern exterior. Designed for construction on a slab.

LARGE LIVING~ROOM WINDOW IN STYLE

$3,700⁰⁰

All prices shown are freight paid within 11 Midwestern States— slightly higher in other areas.

You Get *So Much More* from National Homes!

See for Yourself at
NATION-WIDE OPEN HOUSE!

asbestos shingle roof

*MANY YEARS
BEFORE THE
ASBESTOS
HEALTH HAZARD
SCARE!*

VISIT NATIONAL

*MULTI-PANED
PICTURE
WINDOWS*

55

*ROOM DIVIDERS
POPULAR*

1955 **FORD**

ROW HOUSE (SAN FRANCISCO)

rooms

TRANS-EAST BY WILLETT IN SOLID CHERRY
finest expression of the new Oriental trend in contemporary furniture

PLANK FLOOR

WITH A BeautyQueen KITCHEN!

Something to Be Proud of— YOUR LYON STEEL KITCHEN IN YOUR CHOICE OF COLORS!

A KITCHEN BY St. Charles

AMERICAN ST'D. SINK

55

Antique Copper THE NEWEST FAD

Youngstown Steel Kitchens

BATHROOMS

AVAIL. COLORS

AllianceWare

ALLIANCEWARE, INC. • ALLIANCE, OHIO   Bathtubs • Lavatories • Closets • Sinks

AMERICAN-STANDARD

American-Standard Bathroom

SMALL "DENTAL" SINK

BATHROOM SINKS BUILT INTO VANITY CABINETS BECOMING A NEW TREND. (ABOVE)

NEO~ANGLE TUB

BRIGGS

55

The WATER CLOSET that FLUSHES POLITELY

CASE FOUNDED 1853

We invite you to give your home the comfort, protection and beauty of the future chosen for America's finest bathrooms. It's the famous CASE Non-Overflow One-Piece* with the whispering flush. In 32 rich colors and sparkling black and white...the widest vitreous china color selection available...it will blend with any color scheme. Available through plumbing contractors everywhere. Ask your Case distributor or write W. A. Case & Son Mfg. Co., 33 Main Street, Buffalo 3, N. Y.

Case

AVAIL. IN 32 COLORS!

VANITY SINK

note THE VARIETY OF CRANE LAVATORY SINK STYLES

CRANE CO. FOUNDED JULY 4, 1855

CRANE'S CENTENNIAL ANNIVERSARY YEAR!

Cunningham

TOILETS and LAVATORIES

Designed especially for trailer homes... Cunningham fixtures will provide years of satisfaction and trouble-free service because they're built to the highest standards. Cunningham quality costs no more... so look for the name ...ask for the industry's leading bathroom fixtures by name. It is your guarantee of complete satisfaction.

"JET" Unit
• Exclusive, quiet jet flushing action
• Compact...attractive...passes all municipal, state, federal codes
• Beautiful top quality white vitreous china...finest fittings

LAVATORY
• Extra Capacity bowl
• Anti-splash rim
• Built-in overflow protection
• Wide shelf with glass and soap receptacles
• Deep skirt—more attractive appearance

Cunningham Mermaid
Established 1838

Write for illustrated catalogs today.

James Cunningham Son & Co., Inc.
ESTABLISHED 1838
ROCHESTER 8, NEW YORK

SUITABLE FOR MOBILE HOMES OR CONVENTIONAL HOUSES.

WIDESPREAD POPULARITY OF COLOR FIXTURES IN MID~1950s REFLECTS PROSPEROUS ERA.

ELJER

DIVISION OF THE MURRAY CORPORATION OF AMERICA

ELJER

...Why Wait'?

when a **GERBER** second bathroom costs so little

MFD. IN CHICAGO

KOHLER OF KOHLER SINCE 1873

MFD. IN KOHLER, WI.

KOHLER BATHROOM FIXTURES
Cosmopolitan Bath . . . . Gramercy Lavatory

55

It's a Bathroom by **RICHMOND**

MFD. IN METUCHEN, N.J.

(A REYNOLDS ALUMINUM SUBSIDIARY)

WILSHIRE SINK
Two compartments...Two work surface

KOHLER

note HORIZONTALLY ~ SLATTED "JALOUSIE" WINDOW BY THIS KITCHEN SINK.

colors of gleaming Universal-Rundle
Choose Azure Blue, Desert Tan,
Verdant Green, Arctic White or Mist Gray —

MFD. IN NEW CASTLE, PA.

HELPFUL BOOK tells how you can plan lovely rooms with fixtures!

Universal ~ RUNDLE

U/R gives you style and quality backed by 54 years

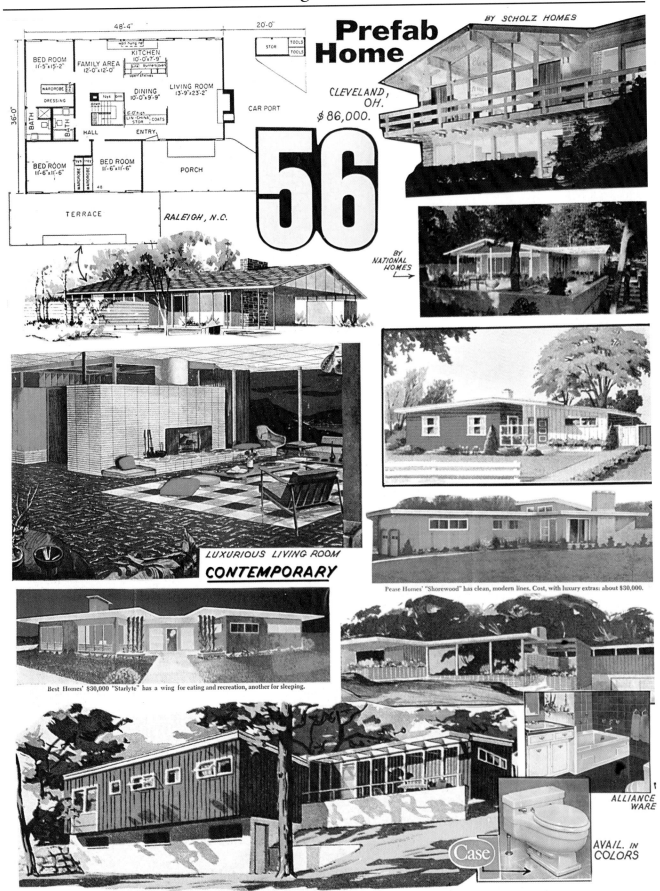

Prefab Home

BY SCHOLZ HOMES

CLEVELAND, OH. $86,000.

56

RALEIGH, N.C.

BY NATIONAL HOMES

LUXURIOUS LIVING ROOM

CONTEMPORARY

Pease Homes' "Shorewood" has clean, modern lines. Cost, with luxury extras: about $30,000.

Best Homes' $30,000 "Starlyte" has a wing for eating and recreation, another for sleeping.

ALLIANCE WARE

AVAIL. IN COLORS

Case

ALADDIN Readi-Cut

THE ALADDIN COMPANY
BAY CITY, MICH.

ALADDIN HOUSES ARE NOT PREFABRICATED

BUILD IT YOURSELF

WORLD'S LARGEST MANUFACTURER OF READI-CUT HOMES

NEW HOME DESIGNS FOR 1956!

the new Nationals

One in every seven new homes this year will be factory-built.

"LIBERTY" HOME

MFD. BY

LEWIS MANUFACTURING CO.

1262 Lafayette Ave.   Bay City, Mich.

2 bedrooms — $4610

2 bedrooms — $3952

3 bedrooms — $5378

3 bedrooms — $5898

56

POPULAR RANCH STYLES

WITH WOOD PANELING

WITH CRANK-OUT VERTICAL PANES, new ALUMINUM-FRAME WINDOWS POPULAR IN THE WEST

PACIFIC GROVE, CA.

IN OKLAHOMA ✳

PORTLAND CEMENT ASSOCIATION

ADVERTISED THE ADVANTAGES OF BUILDING WITH CONCRETE WALLS and SUB~FLOORS.

CAPE COD STYLE

IN ILLINOIS ✳

✳ = BUILT WITH
Concrete

COLONIAL

IN GEORGIA ✳

houses

TRADITIONAL SUBURBAN

IN WASHINGTON ✳

57

RANCH STYLES POPULAR IN MANY REGIONS.

IN MICHIGAN ✳

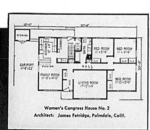

Women's Congress House No. 2
Architect: James Fetridge, Palmdale, Calif.

FEATURING AN EAT-IN KITCHEN, FAMILY ROOM and EXTRA ½~BATH

(CELOTEX BUILDING PRODUCTS USED)

DESIGNED FROM COLLECTIVE IDEAS AT FEDERAL HOUSING ADMINISTRATOR ALBERT M. COLE'S "WOMEN'S CONGRESS ON HOUSING," A NATIONAL MEETING IN WASHINGTON, D.C.

IN CALIFORNIA

RANCH STYLE

TRADITIONAL

IN IOWA ✳

MODERNISTIC

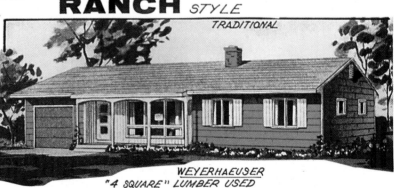

WEYERHAEUSER "4 SQUARE" LUMBER USED

(RT.) CONCRETE HOME

IN COLORADO

PARTIAL BRICK CONSTRUCTION

VARIOUS CONTEMPORARY STYLES

BETTER HOMES and GARDENS "IDEA HOME" OF 1957

PARTIALLY-ENCLOSED CARPORT (ABOVE)

BED

BED

1/2 BATH

BATH

DINING (AREA)

8 x 8

KITCH

FP

LIVING ROOM

BED

57

GRAPE-STAKE FENCE

POPULAR DURING THIS ERA

IN CALIFORNIA

ADOBE BRICK WALLS and CHIMNEY (ABOVE)

WALLS OF GLASS FOR INDOOR-OUTDOOR LIVING

CAR: 1957 OLDSMOBILE

UNDER CONSTRUCTION

SPLIT-LEVEL

VARIOUS CONTEMPORARY STYLES

HOUSE BELOW HAS SLIDING GLASS PATIO DOORS AT REAR (ARROW)

- No old-fashioned protruding cranks or levers.
- Sealed ball bearings and adjustable nylon rollers assure whisper quiet operation of doors.
- Available in all sizes, complete with glass and screens, from leading lumber yards and building supply dealers.

VISIBLE EVIDENCE OF QUALITY CONSTRUCTION

Manufactured by
KENDALL-ADDINGTON, INC.

Fresno 6, Calif.
265 Divisadero   Tel: AM 4-3063

Sacramento 15, Calif.
1655 E. El Camino Tel: WA 2-5060

Now — at last — you can purchase sliding glass windows and doors as complete units from one manufacturer, assembled with double-strength glass in windows; full frame, non-corrosive screens, head drips and window sills.

Two panes of glass

Blanket of dry air insulates window

"Living With A View"

A BETTER BUY... *Thermopane* !

Bondermetic (metal-to-glass) Seal
Keeps air dry and clean

CONTINUED GROWING POPULARITY OF WIDE GLASS SLIDING DOORS, OFTEN LEADING TO BACK YARD, TERRACE OR PATIO.

DUAL-PANE GLASS (AS SEEN AT RIGHT)

120 Modern READI-CUT PLANS
5 to 8 Rooms from $3,000
WE PAY THE FREIGHT
RANCH • TWO-STORY
COLONIAL • CAPE COD
ALADDIN READI-CUT HOMES

MAIL COUPON TO:
The ALADDIN CO., Bay City, Mich.

KIT~BUILT HOUSES

ALADDIN READI-CUT HOUSES ARE ENGINEERED TO SAVE YOU THOUSANDS OF DOLLARS!

BUILD IT YOURSELF!—Aladdin designed and manufactured the first Readi-Cut Home over 50 years ago. Tens of thousands of people have discovered how easy it is to build an Aladdin. Our customers have saved thousands of dollars by doing part or all of the work themselves. **NOT PREFABRICATED**—The lumber is cut to fit by precision machines, ready to be nailed in place. Each piece is marked and shown on our erection drawings. **QUALITY**—All materials...lumber, doors, windows, flooring, paint, hardware ... everything furnished are highest quality. Not only do you save—your finished Aladdin Home will be a joy to behold—beautifully designed and solidly constructed to meet the highest building standards. **CATALOG**—Send for Aladdin's handsome new catalog now and you will understand how Aladdin can save you up to 30 or 40% on your new home.

57

LEVITTOWN

"PENNSYLVANIAN" 1½-STORY MASS~PRODUCED TRACT HOUSE BUILT BY LEVITT and SONS CONSTRUCTION CORP., LEVITTOWN, PA. 5 STYLES AVAIL. 4 BEDROOMS and ALL~ELECTRIC KITCHEN

$14,500. and up, INCLUDING 70' x 100' LANDSCAPED LOT.

western~STYLE FAMILY ROOM

(*new 1957 "COSCO"* CONTEMPORARY FURNITURE ILLUSTRATED)

LOUVRES BELOW WINDOWS CAN BE EITHER FAUX OR ACTUALLY SERVE FOR VENTILATION.

Today's smartest floors wear **KENTILE**®

↑ NARROW
GALLERY~
KITCHEN
LOOKS OUT ONTO
PATIO.
(ADJACENT
EATING AREA
SHOWN IN
BACKGROUND.)

WHITEWASHED
BRICK ↓

BEDROOM/STUDY (PANELED WALLS)

Interiors

BETTER~GRADE DOORS

LIGHTWEIGHT, HOLLOW
PLYWOOD~
VENEER DOORS
FREQUENTLY
USED IN
INEXPENSIVE
HOMES.

MASONITE® PRODUCTS

57

SOLID DOORS
ARE OF BEST
QUALITY. →

PLAIN
MODERN~
STYLE
FIREPLACE
WITHOUT
A
MANTEL
OR
EXTENDED
HEARTH
(CARPETING SO
CLOSE TO OPEN
FIREPLACE IS A
SAFETY
HAZARD.)

Well dressed
for any occasion...

flush doors faced with Masonite Dorlux panels

KITCHENS

BUILT~IN APPLIANCES
GROWING IN POPULARITY (AS ARE
INTERCOMS AND
VARIOUS *ELECTRICAL GADGETS.*)

An eyeful of easier living by WIZARD

Wizard Kitchen
Designed by
Parker Heath

Wizard
Automatic Washer
Gets Even "Clean"
Clothes Cleaner

57 WASHER DRYER

Tappan's Fabulous Electronic cuts cooking time 90%!—
potatoes in 4 minutes, roasts in 30 minutes
perfectly. Write for complete information and price.

† Trade Mark Reg. & Patents Pending

ONLY **GAS**
does so much more...

ANCESTOR TO THE MODERN
MICROWAVE OVEN!

Honeywell
First in Controls

new "DAY~NITE" ROUND
THERMOSTAT BY
MINNEAPOLIS ~ HONEYWELL
(ADDITIONAL MODELS, LOWER RT.)

Honeywell Thermostats

Electric Clock Thermostat
turns heating or cooling up
or down automatically—at
any desired times.

Golden Circle, for heating,
cooling. Works with out-
door thermostat for Elec-
tronic Moduflow® comfort.

Honeywell Round, world's
largest-selling thermostat
for heating. Accurate as a
fine watch.

Year-Round Thermostat
controls heating and cooling; gives finger-tip control
of either.

Tappan de luxe electric Built-in gives double-oven convenience. Bake and
broil at the same time! Top oven is fully automatic, chrome-lined for easy
cleaning. Illuminated, eye-level control panel. Surface unit has four Tappan
super-speed elements plus built-in griddle. Easy and economical to install.

ELECTRIC
TAPPAN GOLD RIBBON RANGE

ELJER *FIXTURES*

ELJER MAGIC . . . *helps change "For Sale" signs to "Sold"*

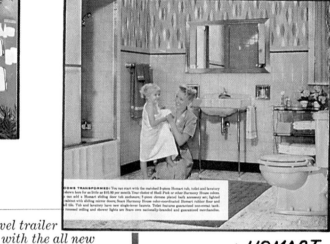

ROOMS TRANSFORMED! You can start with the matched 3-piece Homart tub, toilet and lavatory shown here for as little as $15.00 per month Your choice of Shell Pink or other Harmony House colors. You can add a Homart sliding door tub enclosure; 7-piece chrome plated bath accessory set; lighted cabinet with sliding mirror doors; Sears Harmony House color-coordinated Homart rubber floor and wall tile. Tub and lavatory have new single-lever faucets. Toilet features guaranteed non-sweat tank; rimmed ceiling and shower lights are Sears own nationally-branded and guaranteed merchandise.

(ABOVE) **HOMART** *FIXTURES IN "SHELL PINK" (SEARS, ROEBUCK: DISTRIBUTOR)*

BY MID~ 1950s, MOST MOBILE HOME PLUMBING FIXTURES ARE HOUSE TYPE, THOUGH THIS TYPE CONTINUES IN MANY SMALL TRAVEL TRAILERS and MOTOR HOMES.

MODERNIZE *your travel trailer with the all new*

SWIRL-O-WAY TRAILER TOILET
Only 17½″ front-to-back

Space saving size, easy installation makes the Swirl-O-Way your best buy for modification or modernization. Compact, pull-man-type operation for trouble-free service and low upkeep.

Features: standard trailer size seat; rugged vitreous china bowl; rust-proof, long wearing polished aluminum body; 3-inch waste opening; 10½-inch rough-in. *Plus* famous Watts vacuum breaker.

See your local dealer or trailer supply store

Swirl-O-Way

Manufactured by
WELLENS MANUFACTURING CO.
3809 W. Jefferson Blvd., Los Angeles 16, Calif.

57

U/R New Trend Fixtures for home, institutional, commercial and industrial use

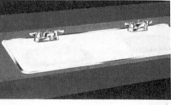

The Dulavoir—*new twin basin cast iron counter top lavatory, the answer to bathroom "bottlenecks." Available in U/R colors and Arctic White.*

The Uni-Dial Lavatory—*offers one hand control of water temperature and volume. In U/R colors and Arctic White.*

HOPPER~TYPE TRAILER, TRAIN and MARINE TOILET SIMILAR TO SOME USED IN HOMES UP TO THE 1880s, BUT REFINED in CONSTRUCTION. CAN BE USED in MODERN HOMES to CONSERVE WATER. ✳ FUNNEL~SHAPED BOWL HAS TRAPDOOR AT BOTTOM WHICH OPENS DURING THE FLUSHING ACTION.

Universal  **Rundle**
MAKER OF THE WORLD'S FINEST PLUMBING FIXTURES
Plants in Camden, N. J.; Milwaukee, Wis.; New Castle, Pa.; Redlands, Calif.; Hondo, Texas

✳=EXCEPT WHERE PROHIBITED BY LOCAL BUILDING CODES

PEBBLE BEACH, CA.

ALADDIN HOMES
BAY CITY, MI.

↑
MIDWESTERN
OUTSIDE~
ENTRANCE
CELLAR

1958 DE SOTO

honey-sweet home

GREENDALE, WIS.

HULA~HOOP
FAD!

INCREASED PUBLIC
INTEREST IN
MOBILE HOMES and

TRAILERS

"RECESSION"--
A YEAR OF BUSINESS DOWNTURN

58

BORG ~ WARNER'S
INGERSOLL ~ HUMPHREYES
FIXTURES
(SINCE 1882)

ALADDIN "READI-CUT" HOMES = $3000. up
Noted for HIGHEST QUALITY and BEST CONSTRUCTION

1958 EDSEL

NEW! Correlated decorative tile of
Oriental Motif

INDOOR
AIR CONDITIONING
SYSTEM IN CELLAR
RECREATION ROOM

STACKABLE
DRYER
ABOVE
WASHER
(WESTINGHOUSE
"SPACE MATES")

HERMOSA TILE

During the past 53 years Aladdin has sold more Readi-Cut Homes than any other pre-cut house manu-

Choice of 115 Modern Floor Plans to $10,000

ALADDIN READI-CUT HOMES

THE ALADDIN COMPANY, Bay City, Michigan

facturer. Aladdin Readi-Cut Homes have been built in all 49 states and 38 countries.

SARASOTA, FL.

Prefab House Has Aluminum Exterior
AND ROOF

CHERRYHILL WEST

SUNNYVALE, CA.

NEWARK, CA.

Lido Faire

Everyone's moving up to CEDAR SHAKES and SHINGLES

Honeywell

Electric Clock Thermostat
Automatically turns heating or cooling up or down at the desired time daily for extra comfort and economy.

H First in Control

Heating-Cooling Thermostat
Controls both heating and cooling. Changes from one to the other— automatically.

"DAY~ NITE ROUND"

ROBERTSHAW wall thermostat

GM FRIGIDAIRE
Built and Backed by General Motors

BUILT-IN WALL OVEN

AMERICAN-Standard
PLUMBING AND HEATING DIVISION

WALL-HUNG BOWL and TANK

rainbow

It's NEW...it's the American-Standard bathroom that's so beautiful, so colorful, so easy to clean

oven & range

Chapter 9   1960-1969

In the 1960s, an increased prosperity in the United States made possible a return to diversity in house styles and the appearance of more luxuries. Unlike the 1950s, the '60s showed a variety of styles more typical of the 1930s—colonial, Spanish-Mediterranean, ranch styles, contemporary, traditional, split-levels, and bi-levels. But, as in the 1950s, each style became less distinct, so houses of this decade looked more and more alike.

This chapter mentions three styles that reappear on the American house scene after long absences. One is the mansard roof, comprising the top floor of a two-story house. Another is a multi-faceted house, an echo of the octagon-house fad that swept across mid-nineteenth century America. The last is an "engawa" (Japanese covered porch), which shows a renewed interest in Oriental styles. Another example of what may be a trend toward idiosyncratic shapes is a wine-tank house—large, round and short, with a low-pitched conical roof and exposed rafter ends.

Now that most necessities were affordable and indeed possessed by most Americans who wanted them, manufacturers began producing and advertising more luxuries. These included myriad variations on the necessities: gated entryways to yards, courtyards, walled gardens, backyard swimming pools, patios, indoor/outdoor living rooms, sunken living rooms, "Thai teak floors," "mezzanine dining rooms," family rooms, rec[reational] rooms, two-sink bathrooms, sunken tubs/showers, bathroom/dressing rooms with theater lights around the mirrors, bathroom fixtures in different colors and shapes and with ridges and other decorative details.

Then there were entirely new items: colored plastic telephones, cabanas or storage sheds, portable dishwashers, "gallery kitchens," single-lever faucets, one-piece molded fiberglass shower/bathtub stalls, two-car garages, garage door openers, saunas, skylights and translucent light-panels, hanging and free-standing fireplaces, and decorative concrete blocks for garden walls.

Thousands of Aladdin Readi-Cut Homes, built 50 years ago, are sound.

ALADDIN "READY-CUT" KIT HOUSES

THE ALADDIN COMPANY, Bay City, Michigan

THERMOSTAT IMPROVED

HONEYWELL CONTROLS

COOL OFF HEAT

New Weather Station

Choice of 115 designs

A smart *master* control for your year-round air conditioning system. You'll control the temperature, check humidity, barometer, and indoor-outdoor temperatures. Pre-set automatic temperature changes. Warning lights signal "clogged filter" and other minor disorders you can correct.

Liberty Home

RANCH STYLES

THE AMHERST

60

PARAGON HOME
(KIT)

THE KIRKLIN $4122
6 Rooms
3 Bedroom Ranch

New Indoor-Outdoor System

BY HONEYWELL

DFPA TESTED QUALITY **Fir Plywood***

PLASTIC TRANS-LUCENT PATIO ROOF

UNLIMITED *from* **ALSYNITE**

CONTEMPORARY

"STOR-IT" STORAGE SHED

CALIFORNIA CABANAS and STOR-IT-ROOMS

FOR USE WITH EITHER MOBILE OR WITH ANY CONVENTIONAL HOMES

MOBILE HOME (WITH SKIRTING TO HIDE HITCH and WHEELS)

TRANSLUCENT CEILING PANELS

Modern

Kitchens

Traditional

GENERAL ELECTRIC DISHWASHERS

60

"MOBILE MAID" PORTABLE

"EARLY AMERICAN" KITCHEN DECOR

4½ minutes after dessert you're done!

PLASTIC PHONES in COLORS

There's **AllianceWare** bathroom luxury for everyone in...

T~SHAPED SIDE MOLDING ON ALLIANCE TUB

bath.

SINGLE~LEVER FAUCET

DUAL FAUCETS "CONTOUR" TUB

60

bathrooms

THIS SIDE OF TUB BACKS TO A WALL

"RESTAL" TUB

AMERICAN~STANDARD

It's NEW...It's **American-Standard** *PLUMBING AND HEATING DIVISION*

"NORWALL" WALL-HUNG W.C.

"CADET" W.C. GETS ROUNDED~FRONT PEDESTAL

NEW OFF-CENTER LAVATORY,

the Sherrilyn, is a high-style, high-quality fixture with the beautiful, flowing lines that will excite model home visitors. Note the wide side ledge that gives the space of a counter top for holding toiletries and other articles. The deep, roomy bowl has both anti-splash rim and hidden front overflow. The Sherrilyn is vitreous china in color or white, 24" x 20".

CHURCH SEAT and cover snap off, without removing hinge posts, for easy cleaning. Modern seat is smartly designed and has a streamlined cover. Both of high-impact plastic in white and colors.

New Ledgewood lavatory (shown)

"CRESCENT" SINK

"WALSAN" W.C.

BRIGGS *BEAUTYWARE*

CRANE

luxury of Crane *at open and close with a quarter turn*

SILENTO WATER CLOSET of vitreous china is a wall-hung, syphon jet model featuring quiet action. Available in six compatible colors.

KILMER LAVATORY of vitreous china for counter-top installations. It has twin concealed front overflows, anti-splash rim, deep contour bowl. Choice of colors or white.

"CRITERION" TUB

CRANE

CONTEMPORARY

CURTITIONS

Pella WOOD FOLDING DOORS

MAKE EXTRA ROOMS WITH WOOD FOLDING DOORS

ASIAN INFLUENCE IN DESIGN

JAPANESE STYLE "ENGAWA" (COVERED PORCH)

HANGING FIREPLACE

61

POOLSIDE LIVING

SWIMMING POOLS OFTEN FENCED OFF, WHEN THERE ARE TODDLERS PRESENT.

PASS~THRU KITCHENS IN STYLE (ALSO SEE ILLUSTRATIONS AT UPPER LEFT)

CONTEMPORARY SALT LAKE CITY

HOUSE BELOW, AS IT LOOKED WHEN UNDER CONSTR. IN 1961 →

61

MORE RECENT VIEW

A-FRAME HOUSE

REC. ROOM

1961 INTERNATIONAL "TRAVELALL"

HALLWAY WITH BUILT-IN DRAWERS, CABINETS, STORAGE CLOSETS

UNDER CONSTR.

MONTEREY, CA.

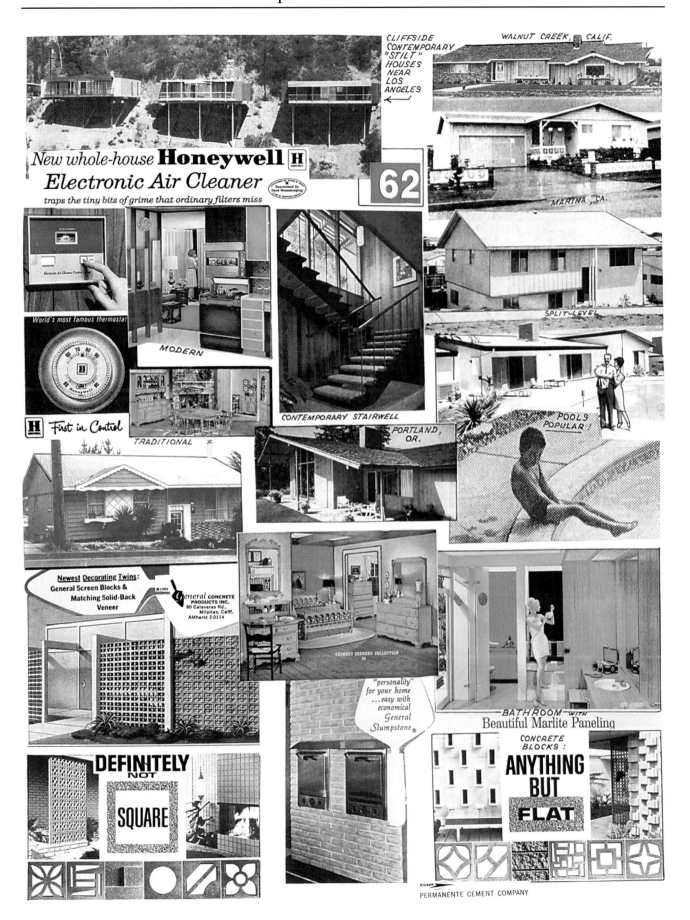

SPLIT-LEVEL

PORTOLA VALLEY, CA.

RANCH STYLE

MESA PALOS VERDES, CA.

CONCORD, CA.

WESTERN STYLE

ISE 1963 Merit Award
HOMES
63

PALO DEL AMO, CA.

SAN FRANCISCO

RANCH-STYLE TRACT HOUSE

CONTEMPORARY

Keystone Non-Climbable Fence

ROW HOUSE

ASIAN STYLE

MODERN-DAY "CAPE COD"

RIO DEL MAR, CA.

SEATTLE

SAN RAFAEL, CA.

MILL VALLEY, CA.

SOME UNCONVENTIONAL SHAPES APPEAR

PRE-FAB.

This is the frame for a steel-framed house

BETHLEHEM STEEL

BETHLEHEM STEEL

3 ABOVE HOUSES ARE OF STEEL-FRAME CONSTRUCTION.

"WINE TANK" HOUSE

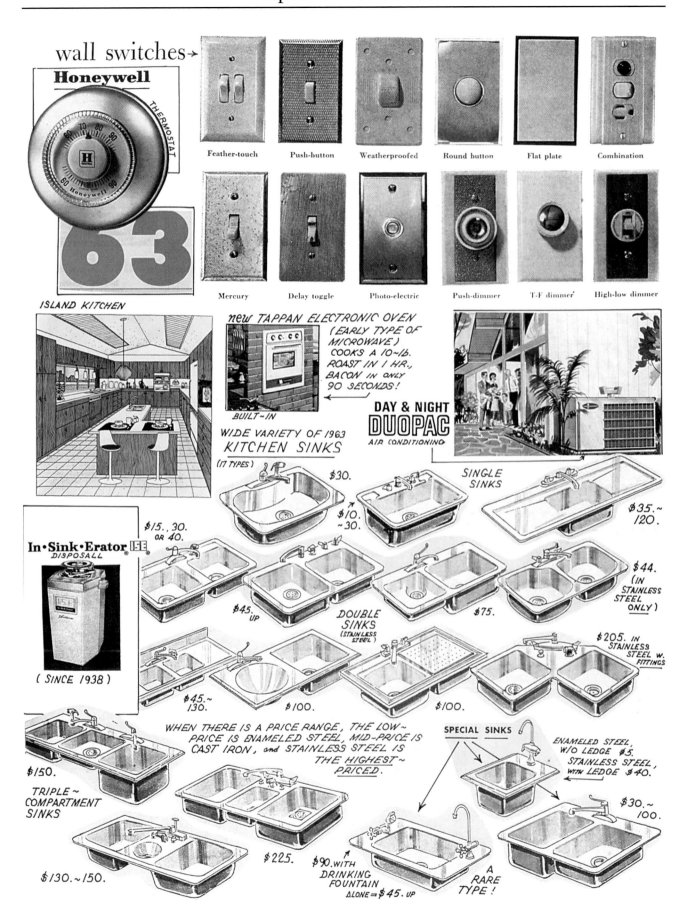

wall switches→

Honeywell

THERMOSTAT

63

Feather-touch   Push-button   Weatherproofed   Round button   Flat plate   Combination

Mercury   Delay toggle   Photo-electric   Push-dimmer   T-F dimmer   High-low dimmer

ISLAND KITCHEN

new TAPPAN ELECTRONIC OVEN
(EARLY TYPE OF
MICROWAVE)
COOKS A 10~lb.
ROAST IN 1 HR.,
BACON IN ONLY
90 SECONDS!

BUILT~IN

DAY & NIGHT
DUOPAC
AIR CONDITIONING

WIDE VARIETY OF 1963
KITCHEN SINKS
(17 TYPES)

$30.

SINGLE
SINKS

$10.
~30.

$35.~
120.

In•Sink•Erator ISE
DISPOSALL

$15., 30.
OR 40.

$44.
(IN
STAINLESS
STEEL
ONLY)

$45.
UP

DOUBLE
SINKS
(STAINLESS
STEEL)

$75.

$205. IN
STAINLESS
STEEL w.
FITTINGS

(SINCE 1938)

$45.~
130.

$100.

$100.

WHEN THERE IS A PRICE RANGE, THE LOW~
PRICE IS ENAMELED STEEL, MID~PRICE IS
CAST IRON, and STAINLESS STEEL IS
THE HIGHEST~
PRICED.

SPECIAL SINKS

ENAMELED STEEL,
W/O LEDGE $5.
STAINLESS STEEL,
WITH LEDGE $40.

$150.

TRIPLE~
COMPARTMENT
SINKS

$30.~
100.

$130.~150.

$225.

$90. WITH
DRINKING
FOUNTAIN
ALONE = $45. UP

A
RARE
TYPE !

TOWN or COUNTRY

Now is the time to add the warmth and pleasure of a *FREE~STANDING FIREPLACE*
FireHood (AVAIL. IN 9 COLORS)

STACKABLE WASHER and DRYER IN KITCHEN CLOSET

SAUNA

Viking Sauna is the world's leader in Sauna sales. 50,000 installations!

Take care in the Sauna you choose. And especially the heater/dehumidifier. It is the most important part...the heart...of your Sauna.

Viking Sauna's all electric heater with circulating fan means savings, quality, incomparable performance eliminating need for costly plumbing (gas lines, flues, drains). IMPORTED and built of highest quality Swedish stainless steel to last a lifetime! Heats in a jiffy—up to 70% faster than other units, your Viking Sauna electric heater/dehumidifier is easily installed, unconditionally guaranteed, listed with Underwriters' Laboratories.

Write or call your Viking Sauna Dealer for information and free brochure.

Viking Sauna

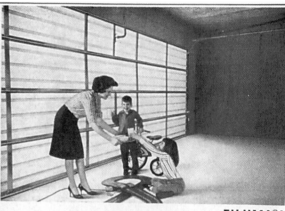

Turn your garage into a Fun Room...with FILUMA®!
TRANSLUCENT GARAGE DOOR

DELTA®
SINGLE HANDLE BALL FAUCETS

Good Housekeeping

COMMENDED by PARENTS' MAGAZINE

The Lavatory model by Delta has mirror depth chrome and simple lines assuring beauty and lasting ease of cleaning.

Insist on Delta . . . the faucet with only ONE moving part . . . "A compliment to any home."

There are over 400 model applications of Delta Faucets.

DELTA
FAUCET CORPORATION
GREENSBURG, INDIANA

AVAILABLE

BATHRM. SKYLIGHTS →

KOHLER

Kohler makes the kind of bath tub— *"DYNAMETRIC" WITH INSIDE RE-SHAPED FOR COMFORT*

SEARS, ROEBUCK FIXTURES

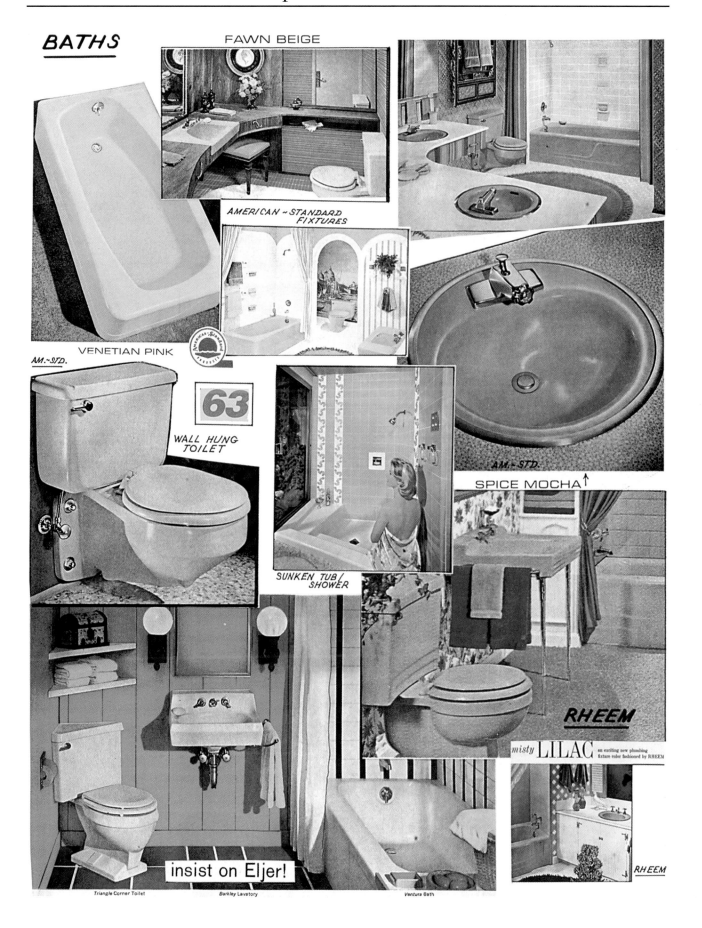

BATHS

FAWN BEIGE

AMERICAN ~ STANDARD FIXTURES

VENETIAN PINK

AM.~STD.

63

WALL HUNG TOILET

AM.~STD.

SPICE MOCHA ↑

SUNKEN TUB / SHOWER

RHEEM

misty LILAC an exciting new plumbing fixture color fashioned by RHEEM

RHEEM

insist on Eljer!

Triangle Corner Toilet   Barkley Lavatory   Ventura Bath

PEBBLE BEACH
CALIFORNIA

GATED ENTRY TO PROPERTY
AT
UPPER LEFT

ABOVE 1964~BLT. HOUSE TORN DOWN IN RECENT YEARS SO AN EVEN LARGER HOUSE COULD TAKE ITS PLACE!

64

SPLIT~ LEVEL

RANCH~STYLE HOMES (WOOD AND STUCCO)

CONTEMPORARY~STYLE LIVING ROOM (SEMI~FORMAL)

CRATE

KOHLER GREEN

NEAR THE END OF ERA WHEN NEW FIXTURES WERE SHIPPED IN WOODEN CRATES ... NOW SHIPPED IN CARDB'D. BOXES.

(2 VIEWS OF SAME HOUSE)

NOTE THE ENCLOSED COURTYARD

LAVATORY SINK

KOHLER FITTINGS
Beauty you'll love to live with
(All-Brass quality that lasts a lifetime)

KOHLER of KOHLER

KOHLER YELLOW

(OTHER BRANDS ON NEXT PG.)

65

PEBBLE BEACH

MARINA, CA.

2 ~ CAR GARAGE USUALLY ATTACHED at FRONT OF HOUSE.

SKYLIGHTS GROW IN POPULARITY

(VARIOUS TYPES ILLUSTRATED)

HERMOSA TILE

GARDEN BATH

"BUTTERFLY" CARPORT

STORAGE IN CENTER SECTION

BELOW: ILLUSTRATED COLOR COMBINATION = EXPRESSO with SUEZ TAN

Kohler color with a decorator surprise —lavatories in new accent shades

COUNTRY STYLE

ARIZONA ADOBE

CAPE COD →

RANCH STYLE

MONTEREY COLONIAL

SPLIT-LEVEL ↓

66

MODEL HOMES AT THE NEW SKYLINE FOREST SUBDIVISION, MONTEREY, CA.

CONTEMPORARY

PEBBLE BEACH, CA.

ALADDIN READI-CUT **HOMES**

Offers:
★ New Quick-erect System
★ Custom Manufacturing
★ Quality Homes for Less
WE PAY THE FREIGHT

COLONIAL

CENTER COURTYARD FLORIDA

KENTILE VINYL FLOOR

VINYL LINOLEUM FLOORS ARE EMBOSSED TO LOOK LIKE BRICK (ABOVE)

ALADDIN READI-CUT KIT HOMES BAY CITY, MI.

1966 PLANS AVAILABLE FOR THESE:↓

125 1½ and 2-STORY HOMES
Traditional and Contemporary Styles

100 MULTI-LEVEL HOMES
Split-Levels • Hillsides • Bi-Levels

100 ONE-STORY HOMES
From 1600 to 2800 Square Feet

130 ONE-STORY HOMES
Under 1600 Sq. Ft.—Modest Budgets

KWIKSET LOCKSET

AMERICA'S LARGEST-SELLING RESIDENTIAL LOCKSET

AVOCADO-COLORED BUILT-INS

Choose **DeVAC**
THERMO-BARRIER* WINDOWS

HEAT FLOWS EVENLY THROUGHOUT ROOM

Hunter Electric
HEATLINER BASEBOARD

New Hunter
Bathroom **TRIO**

HEATS, LIGHTS, VENTILATES

One remarkable unit does all three!

Now enjoy comfortable warmth, plenty of light and fast removal of steam and odors thru the recessed TRIO from Hunter. Grille frame is stainless steel. Quiet, electrically reversible fan ventilates through 4" duct, which has back-draft damper. Operates from wall switch.

Backed by Hunter's 80-year experience

The range that stands alone...JENN-AIR

SELF-VENTILATING

EXTERIOR C

EXTERIOR D

EXTERIOR E

3 EXTERIOR DESIGNS FOR THE FLOOR PLAN BELOW

PAN-ABODE CUSTOM PRE-CUT CEDAR HOMES

KIT HOUSE

Woodland Homes are entirely pre-cut, at the two Pan-Abode factories.

Barcelona   5 Bedrooms, 3 Baths

FAMILY ROOM · DINING ROOM · KITCHEN · LAUNDRY · PORCH · BATH 3 · W · D

LIVING ROOM · BEDROOM 5 OR DEN · CL. · STORAGE

ENTRY · PORCH · GARAGE

BEDROOM 3 · WARD · BATH 2 · WARD · BEDROOM 2 · BATH 1

HALL · DOWN

BEDROOM 4 · CL. · CL. · BEDROOM 1

IN SACRAMENTO, CA.

67

STONE FIREPLACE

PEBBLE BEACH, CA.

ISLAND KITCHEN with DINING NOOK

KENTILE FLOOR

SKYLIGHTS ABOVE SLATS

Swim in a pool

INNER PATIO

SOME SUBDIVISIONS OFFER A COMMUNITY SWIMMING POOL FOR THE RESIDENTS. PRIVATE POOLS ALSO BECOMING MORE AFFORDABLE.

GALLERY KITCHEN

AVOCADO GREEN FIXTURES (new)

Home at Whispering Palms, Rancho Santa Fe, California

KOHLER OF KOHLER

THE BOLD LOOK

HEAT and LIGHT FROM CEILING GRILLE

HALL · SH. · TUB · W.C.

TO MASTER BEDROOM · BENCH

SH. · TUB · W.C. · BENCH

COMBINATION DRESSING ROOM / COMPARTMENT BATHROOM

KINGSBERRY "FRANKLIN" (GEORGIA) COLONIAL

68

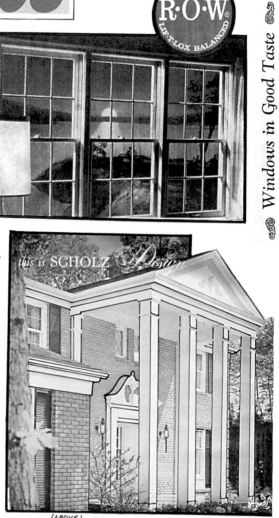

REMOVABLE R·O·W LIF·T·LOX BALANCED

Windows in Good Taste

MULTI-PANED WOOD FRAMED WINDOWS TYPICAL COLONIAL STYLE.

Pella

WOOD STANDARD CASEMENT

WOOD DE LUXE CASEMENT

this is SCHOLZ Design

(ABOVE)
SOUTHERN COLONIAL
TRADITIONAL BRICK

BELOW:
STYLIZED ARTIST'S CONCEPTION, WITH HOUSE WIDTH MUCH EXAGGERATED.

ST. LOUIS, MO.

CAR: 1968 BUICK ELECTRA 225

(WISCONSIN) $34,900.   MODERN SOUTHERN COLONIAL

TRADITIONAL PLAN

EXTERIOR

68

"NEO-COLONIAL"
HIP ROOF CANOPY OVER
PORCH
Materials include red brick, asphalt shingles

BI-LEVEL on SLOPING LOT

IN ST. LOUIS, MO.

OF BRICK, OVER *AT*
PRECAST *GROSSE*
POINTE
CONCRETE *SHORES, MI.*

RANCH-CONTEMPORARY STYLES

SPLIT-LEVEL

a

BEAUMONT Plan 3156 a, b
Tri-level, 4 bedrooms, 3 baths, stepdown living room,
stepdown family room, dining gallery, breakfast nook

b

ABOVE:
IN
PASADENA,
CALIF.

IN
HOUSTON,
TEXAS
→

FRENCH STYLE
(MANSARD ROOF IS
TYPICAL)

CONTEMPORARY
TRI-LEVEL

KIT~BUILT HOUSES

This Big Full Color Book of Homes and Plans Shows You How to Build Your Own Home... and Save!

Don't buy a stapled home when a hand-nailed quality home is available from Aladdin.

- OVER 100 PLANS TO CHOOSE FROM
- CUSTOM MANUFACTURING
- QUICK-ERECT SYSTEM
- QUALITY AND COST CONTROL
- QUALITY HOMES FOR LESS
- OLD-FASHIONED, FRIENDLY, QUALITY SERVICE—OUR POLICY FOR OVER 60 YEARS

The Aladdin Company, 68—1
Bay City, Michigan 48706

BOTH COMPANIES WITH HEADQUARTERS IN BAY CITY, MICH.

INTERNATIONAL MILL & TIMBER CO.
Dept. BHBB   BAY CITY, MICHIGAN

FOLLOW THE "DO-IT-YOURSELF" TREND!

BUILD YOUR OWN HOME... SAVE LABOR COSTS

THIS HOME $6535

With the "Do-It-Yourself" idea taking the country by storm, a large percentage of new homes are being built by the owners themselves with the help of neighbors and friends. Anyone can assemble the popular Sterling Ready-Cut-Homes with their simple, easy to follow plans. Every house is complete with lumber cut-to-fit, numbered and marked, ready to erect . . . roofing, nails, hardware, paint, doors, windows, glass. Freight prepaid. You save all the labor costs and builder's profits. Write today for full details!

Prices do not include carpentry labor, heating, lighting, plumbing and masonry materials.

CHOICE OF 57 DESIGNS PRICED FROM $2295 AND UP

Building Plans also available separately at low cost.

CUT-TO-FIT HOMES CUT BUILDING COSTS

1. You save all of today's high labor costs.
2. You save all of the building contractor's profits.
3. You save all the builder's overhead, insurance, taxes.
4. You save the architect's charges for drawings and plans.
5. You save the usual lumber and material wastes.
6. You save time and costly mistakes in construction.

BUY DIRECT FROM MILL — SAVE MONEY!

Sterling Ready-Cut-Homes are as modern as tomorrow! Designed for comfort, convenience and livability . . . with plenty of closets, picture windows and flower boxes . . . large selection of ranch type and conventional designs.

And most important of all you can Build-It-Yourself and save up to 40% on the total cost. Several easy time payment plans. Decide now to join the parade of enthusiastic Do-It-Yourselfers —

TRACT HOUSES IN SAN JOSÉ, CALIF.

68

120 HILLSIDE HOMES

Tri-level and split-level designs, daylight basements and choice of front or rear entries planned to make the most of view and sloping building sites. Illustrated in full color.

$1.50

PLAN 2006-2
WIDTH 65' DEPTH 30'
AREA 1196 sq. ft.

"Find your dream home in this **LIBRARY of HOME PLAN Books** *and build it for Less!"*

MANY HOMES ALSO DESIGNED FROM PICTURES AND FLOOR PLANS FOUND IN VARIOUS "IDEA BOOKS"

GARAGE DOOR CAN BE CONTROLLED FROM THE CAR.

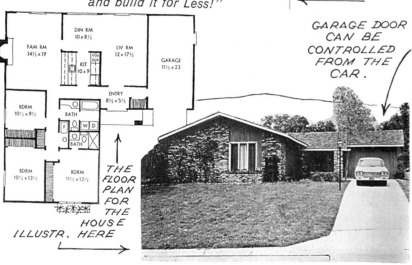

DIN RM 10 x 8½		
FAM RM 14½ x 19	LIV RM 12 x 17½	GARAGE 11½ x 23
KIT 10 x 9		
ENTRY 8½ x 5½		
BDRM 10½ x 9½	BATH	
	F W D	
	BATH	
BDRM 10½ x 13½	BDRM 11½ x 13½	

THE FLOOR PLAN FOR THE HOUSE ILLUSTR. HERE

LARGE UPPER DECK, SLIDING
GLASS PATIO DOORS

INDOOR / OUTDOOR LIVING

"STERLING PARK"

KITCHEN OVERLOOKS
BACKYARD PATIO and
SWIMMING POOL
(SAN JOSÉ, CALIF.)

MEXICAN STYLE, with INNER COURTYARD

1968 Pontiac

68

new $60. FLOATING
SWIMMING POOL ALARM
BLOWS AN AIR HORN
FOR 2½ MINUTES IF
ANYTHING WEIGHING
18 LBS. oR MORE
SHOULD FALL INTO
POOL (WHICH CREATES
WAVES THAT SET OFF
THE ALARM.)

ROOMS, ETC.

SPACE~SAVING
SPIRAL STAIRS WITH
OPEN RISERS
(ABOVE)

68

A **MORGAN**
entranceway adds
beauty, elegance

MEZZANINES

COLONIAL DOUBLE DOORS

MEZZANINE DINING ROOM
OVERLOOKS A DRAMATIC
2~STORY LIVING ROOM

family room (2 FLOOR LEVELS)

IMITATION
SPANISH TILE   **A new Armstrong vinyl floor.**

The Coronelle Collection, by Armstrong.

The floors for the active rooms: vinyl floors by
Armstrong

Tappan You-Shaped Kitchen

CONTEMPORARY

ORIENTAL

One set of cabinets—any decor you like. That's the Tappan You-Shaped idea!

New from Honeywell...

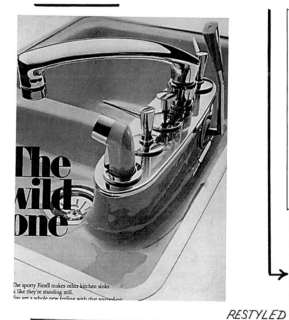

The wild one

The sporty Fiesta makes other kitchen sinks look like they're standing still.

RESTYLED

Thermostats

Honeywell
AUTOMATION

A faucet is just a faucet 'til you get your hand on a Moen.

the faucet

BATHROOMS

TRANSLUCENT CEILING PANELS

CRANE

68

Crane just created a bathtub shaped like people

(for people who just aren't shaped like bathtubs)

new CRANE "EMPRESS" BODY~SHAPED BATHTUB (ABOVE)

Eljer fixtures

"DELRAY" TUB

"EASTON" WALL~ HUNG TOILET

"BRENDA" LAVATORY SINKS →

new "THEATER LIGHTS" BY VANITY OR MIRROR IN BATHROOM ↘

BIDET

KOHLER COLOR FIXTURES

"THE BOLD LOOK OF KOHLER"

MARBLE EFFECTS ON COUNTERS and WALLS

TILE~ENCASED TUB

NEW TRACTS ABOUND

ALLIANCE "GENIE" AUTOMATIC GARAGE DOOR OPENER

CAMBRIDGE, MA.

PARADISE VALLEY, AZ.

Kay Homes

CALIFORNIA

WALLED GARDENS AND BLANK WALLS FACING ADJOINING PROPERTY

69

← 1969 "IDEA HOME" HOUSTON, TX.

MELROSE, MA.

ARCHITECT: Royal Barry Wills & Associates, Boston, Mass.; DEVELOPER: Emil Hanslin Associates, Melrose, Mass.; Cabot's Stains throughout.

Islands Privacy... new idea

EASY-CARE GARDENS

CONTEMPORARY HOMES OF NATURAL WOOD

HONOLULU, HI.

CALIFORNIA

"CURTITION" ROOM DIVIDERS POPULAR

TOWN HOUSES (R.T.)

SPANISH/MEDITERRANEAN STYLE

Pella WOOD FOLDING DOORS

MISSISSIPPI CONDOS (ABOVE)

69

ARIZONA

WORMWOOD PANELING

INDOORS

KOHLER TUB DETAILS

bath CRANE

DETAILS OF VENT DEVICE

RADCLIFFE WATER CLOSET features a ventilating device installed in tank and operated by lifting the flush handle. This starts water flowing through a venturi tube and negative pressure created draws air from bowl, through rim punching and vents, into outlet of bowl. Venting stops when toilet is flushed. Crane Co., 4100 S. Kedzie Ave., Chicago, Ill.

SINKS

Kohler

COLOR: "NEW ORLEANS BLUE"

DUAL ISLAND SINKS

Chapter
10 1970-1980

This final chapter shows two basic conflicting themes. Both continued from the 1960s and even further back. One was propelled by increasing national prosperity and included a busy variety of styles, and an increasing popularity for bigger luxury-filled houses. These latter included five-bedroom houses with over 2300 square feet of space, tri-level houses (one wide-gabled, side-facing design echoed both the New England Saltbox and the Bungaloid styles), two-story houses, triple garages, tall impressive entryways, mezzanines over living rooms or kitchens, and swimming pools, hot tubs, and whirlpools.

In contrast, the second theme emphasized conservation and a return to the Earth. It included log houses with "natural wood" inside and out, decks, woodstoves and fireplaces, solar heating and hot-water systems, water-saving and composting toilets, and double-pane tinted windows. This theme may have been accelerated by the gasoline shortage of 1973, but it also echoed the rustic themes of the 'teens and 1920s. (Even the water-saving toilet dates back to 1939.) One radically different design that fit this theme and became popular during this decade, was the geodesic-dome house invented by American, R. Buckminster Fuller, after World War II. Other house designs that seemed more natural were the A-frame and the chalet, which were often blended in one building.

The 1970s also saw tract houses (now called "housing developments"), kit houses ("modular," "mobile," or "packaged" houses), and duplexes (also called "duet homes"), but other modern more expensive homes were condominiums, townhouses, and gated communities on curving streets and cul-de-sacs (instead of long, straight, neighborhood streets).

Boise Cascade builds them in the nicest places...

SAN JOSE

DUC & ELLIOT'S Kentfield.

3-4-5 BEDROOMS
To 2316 Sq. Ft. **from $43,250⁰⁰**
(ABOVE)

Priced from $22,950.

H. C. ELLIOT HOMES Pleasanton

H. C. ELLIOT

↑ a Ditz-Crane HOME!

From $25,500 to $32,950 VA, FHA & Conventional Fin.

from $24,850 to $26,550

PARK PACIFICA Pacifica   CHALLENGE HOMES INC.

3, 4, 5, 6 Bedrooms from $28,900

SPLIT-LEVEL and 2-STORY HOMES POPULAR, MANY WITH OPEN STAIRWAYS.

TRACT HOME

from $21,200 to $23,300

"LIVING and DINING ROOM CONNECTED"

THE HIGHLANDS Hayward   CHALLENGE HOMES INC.

70

CONTEMPORARY →

MODERN RUSTIC IN NATURAL WOOD ↓

SOBEY ACRES

SARATOGA, CA.

SERRA PARK Westborough   LOEW'S/SNYDER

"DUET HOMES" ↓

homes for today's families

"MEXICAN MODERN" STYLE

from $22,950

MUIR MEADOWS live better for less

MUIR MEADOWS, Unit IV Concord Area

MEDITERRANEAN INFLUENCE

ONE STORY FLOOR PLAN
Available in Single or Two Story Plan

Other Home   Your Home

ANOTHER FINE COMMUNITY BY COSTANZO-WILSON

Priced from $26,950/FHA and VA

PLEASANTON VALLEY

Alamo, Contra Costa County, California

by Levitt & Sons

Levitt & Sons of California, Inc., a Worldwide Service of ITT.

70 CONDOS

ISLANDIA TOWNHOUSES
from $26,500 to $31,400

two and three bedrooms
$16,950 to $19,990

SOME DEVELOPMENTS WITH COMMUNITY POOLS.

Townhouses From $16,950

A new KOHLER FIXTURE COLOR:
Mexican Sand.

FORMICA BRAND
laminate
practical with FORMICA® Panel System 202.
The no-tile bath

Kohler's unique Alterna fittings.

Give Her the Latest Appliance for Christmas...
New Kitchen Convenience

"Gobbles Up" Your Trash and Garbage—Including Bones, Bottles and Cans!

Kenmore COMPACTOR

10-Day FREE Home Demonstration

229⁹⁵

Use Sears Easy Payment Plan

Come to Sears today . . . See the Kenmore Compactor demonstrated!

KOHLER

new STYLE FAUCETS

new Delta Fjord.

DELTA

If your bathroom still looks like a bathroom, it needs the new Delta Fjord.

From $22,200 to $24,500

RANCH STYLES

WEST

SWIMMING POOLS POPULAR IN WARM CLIMATES

DESERT CONTEMPORARY

MODIFIED MONTEREY COLONIAL (WIDE UPPER BALCONY TYPICAL)

1971 Olds Vista-Cruiser: with a built-in observation roof!

71

IN SCOTTSDALE, AZ.

Fun in the sun

MEZZA~NINE OVER LIVING ROOM

INDOOR/ OUTDOOR LIVING

PASS~ THROUGH KITCHEN COUNTER

EXPANSE OF GLASS DOORS OPEN INTO THE BACK YARD. (ABOVE)

MOUNTAIN LAKE DEVELOPMENT →

MEZZANINE and SKYLIGHT OVERLOOKING KITCHEN

McKeon Apartment Homes as low as

$14,195.

CONDOS and PLANNED UNIT DEVELOP~ MENTS (P.U.D.)

WIDE~PORCH RANCH STYLE

71

SPLIT~LEVEL

TWO AND THREE BEDROOM
with two full baths

MEDITERRANEAN ARCHES

ALUMINUM FRAME

Fresh Green. New color from Kohler.
(Now the outdoors look is in.)

It's vibrant. Verdant. Green that goes lush and wild, for the look of a jungle clearing. Or goes sunshine and innocence, to create a spring garden.

Here touches of primeval set off Kohler's semi-sunken Fresh Green Caribbean tub with six feet of stretch-out luxury.

One step up, Kohler's Valencia bidet and boldly sculptured Rochelle toilet. Lady Vanity lavatory, with swing-away spout and spray arm for shampooing.

Kohler Rite-Temp (inset top). Single-control unit maintains water temperature despite changes in water pressure.

Elegant Alterna (inset lower). Style and quick-change versatility. Four accent-inserts with each handle: Teak, Walnut, White, Ebony. Alterna available in chromium or gold electroplate.

THE BOLD LOOK OF KOHLER

whirlpool bath

New Kohler Hydro-Whirl. Non-electric, about $70.

Relax . . . quiet Hydro-Whirl has no motor. Uses no electricity, just water. Bubbly swirls that soothe away aches and tensions . . . stimulating circulation.

CONTEMPORARY (ABOVE) TUSTIN, CA.

Discovery Bay

LIVING ROOM WITH "SOARING CEILING"

Sea Ranch

MUCH USE OF NATURAL WOOD IN CONTEMP. STYLES

RANCH STYLE

NORTHEASTERN COUNTRY STYLE

72

DECKS OF NATURAL WOOD ARE IN STYLE.

MIRRORED DOOR

PPG glass adds beautiful space to your bedroom suite.

KITCHENS.

MOBILE and MODULAR HOME INTERIOR

BLACK BLACK. GREAT COLOR IDEAS BEGIN WITH KOHLER.

SUNKEN TUB

PASS~THROUGH SNACK BAR

CONDOS POPULAR

THE FRONTIER REDWOOD HOME PACKAGE

"RONDO HOME"

TAHOE CITY, CA.

Dramatic beam ceilings

CONDO IN SAN DIEGO, CA.

The source of the radiant heat in Panelectric is heating cable imbedded in each gypsum panel. It transforms electrical energy into radiant heat — safely and in total silence.

Panelectric ceilings warm you like the sun

NuTone's Automatic

73

Garage Door Operator System

Gold Bond RADIANT HEATING SYSTEM

60 70 80

CONTROL

Gold Bond
BUILDING PRODUCTS

SPIRAL STAIRS

hexagon-based

DOME HOUSE

BUBBLE WINDOW

"A-FRAME"

The Birthday bath

BY IRON CRAFT
Since 1927

R
REFORESTATION

THE "NATURAL LOOK" IS "IN!"

new CLAWFOOT TUB!

Kohler celebrates its 100th anniversary with the Birthday Bath. Newest idea from the Bold Craftsmen.

the Klingbeil Company RE-INTRODUCES

homes by EICHLER

ECOLOGY and RECYCLING PROMOTED

CHALLENGER HOMES

18781 N. Highway One, Fort Bragg, CA 95437

FROM $42,950

A New Concept in Packaged Homes
(ABOVE)

KOHLER
100

"HAIDA ~ HIDE HOME, SEATTLE ←

geodesic dome
R. Buckminster Fuller's *DESIGN*
(485 TO 5000 SQ. FT SIZES AVAIL.)

74

CHALETS

BY **CATHEDRALITE DOMES** SANTA CRUZ, CA.

MODULAR HOMES INC., SEATTLE

The Berkeley Craftsmen
2903 Shattuck Ave.
Berkeley, CA 94705
Quality Since 1903

VULCAN by **Viking**
FREE ~ STANDING FIREPLACES IN STYLE

CHARMING PRACTICALITY
BLAZE
Royal Franklin circulating fireplace by Malm

PACIFIC
Quality Glass Door Screens

THE ELEGANT DIFFERENCE
Thermador NI NORRIS INDUSTRIES
A DIVISION OF NORRIS INDUSTRIES
5129 District Blvd., Los Angeles, California 90040

WOODEN SPIRAL STAIRWAY

VARIOUS POOL SHAPES

AMERICAN-STA.

BATH

TRADITIONAL DECOR CONTINUES ALSO

Richard Deacon's Secret Ingredient:
the total cooking convenience of his built-in Thermador Kitchen

AMERICAN STANDARD "MEDITERRANEAN" GOTHIC POOL 6' TUB

LIVING ROOM WITH MEZZANINE ←

PALO ALTO, CA.

FRESNO, L.A., CHICAGO, HOUSTON, SEATTLE and OTHER AREAS

Klingbeil builds on the great Eichler tradition...

7.9% interest while it lasts!

At Los Arboles Addition in Palo Alto

No one has ever hit California home building with such impact as did the first Eichlers introduced way back when. There's been nothing like 'em since, and now The Klingbeil Company carries on in the great Eichler tradition with authentic Eichler contemporary homes designed by Claude Oakland at Los Arboles Addition on Loma Verde and Middlefield in Palo Alto.

Eichlers at Los Arboles Addition present six basic one and two story floor plans with up to 2,500 square feet of living area. Prices start in the low $80,000 range for these spacious four and five bedroom Eichlers, with 7.9% annual interest rates on 80% loans, and no loan fees or prepayment penalties.

It's almost certain that when these Eichlers are sold it will mark the end of an era in Palo Alto.

(1) Eichlers today are bigger and better than ever. Many of the famous Eichler standards are still there. (2) open Atriums. (3) tiled galleries (4) elegant modern kitchens (5) dramatic fireplaces (6) eating areas in the kitchens.

A~FRAME ←

Aquarius In San Mateo

Condominium $52,450. and up

75

MARINA, CA.

SAN FRANCISCO

SAN JOSE, CA.

THE ISLANDS

The Islands

the new award-winning condominium home project in Foster City, Ca.

in San Jose in Sunnyvale.

Williamsburg

MANSARD ROOF

DUTCH COLONIAL REVIVAL

SOUTHERN COLONIAL

Coeur d' Alene

LA JOLLA, CA.

FRENCH STYLE
St. Helena

1976

COUNTRY RANCH STYLE

TRACT HOUSE   SAN JOSE, CA.

Capp
HOMES

CONTEMPORARY

UNDER CONSTRUCTION

MARINA, CA.

Yosemite

NEW ENGLAND "SALTBOX" STYLE

KITCHEN AREAS

(BELOW)
IRON RAILINGS
FREQUENTLY USED
AS ROOM DIVIDERS

a brand
new
very old
idea

SAN JOSE, CA.

REAL LOG HOMES
REAL LOG HOMES INC.
Dept. SM-1, Box 1520, Missoula, Montana 59801
CAROLINA LOG BUILDINGS
Dept. SM-1, Box 363, Fletcher, N. Carolina 28732
VERMONT LOG BUILDINGS
Dept. SM-1, Hartland, Vermont 05048

GATED
ADULT
COMMUNITY
WITH
SECURITY
GUARD
and
GATE
HOUSE →

new AMERI~ CAN~ STD. TUB (ROUND INSIDE) →

BATHS

new "FILLMASTER" FILL VALVE FILLS TANK BY HYDRAULIC PRESSURE and CAN BE SET TO FILL TO DESIRED LEVEL.

OVERFLOW TUBE

TANK (CUT~AWAY VIEW)

WASHDOWN~TYPE TOILETS BECOME OBSOLETE AFTER THE 1960s, AND MOST MFRS. DISCONTINUE THEM DURING THE 1970s.

WASHDOWN TOILET

LIGHTWEIGHT PLASTIC TUB EASILY CARRIED BY ONE MAN.

↑ELJER

Sculptura II, the "water-saving" Toilet

USES 3½ GALS. DROUGHTS IN CALIF. CREATED A DEMAND FOR WATER~ SAVING FIXTURES.

SEARS, ROEBUCK "SCULPTURA" MODELS

AVAIL. COLOR CHOICES (SEARS) ←

Sculptura I Low-Line

new MARBLE~ TONE CHINA FIXTURE

← SIMILAR TYPE AVAIL. FROM UNIVERSAL~ RUNDLE.

new PLASTIC TUB/SHOWER UNIT

Delta & Delex Washerless Faucets
Proudly Crafted in America by Americans

'76

DELTA LAVATORY SINK FAUCET

DELTA MODEL 300 *Single Handle Kitchen Faucet* Flexible hand-held Spray 8" Swing Spout

DELEX LAV. SINK FCT.

DELEX KITCHEN SINK FAUCET

Pleasanton **AMBERWOOD**

NEW! WATER AND ENERGY EFFICIENT HOMES!

Special energy and water efficient features to help conserve our natural resources. Many luxury features included in these one and two story, three and four bedroom floorplans with up to 2½ baths. Prestige location.

no 325 map pg I

Highway 580 to Santa Rita Road to 4485 Sutter Gate Ave.

From $76,990

The **WILLIAM LYON** *Company* **LYON**

EQUAL HOUSING OPPORTUNITY

MILPITAS, CA.

ARCADIA

TALL, IMPRESSIVE ENTRYS POPULAR!

CURVING STREETS and CUL-DE-SACS IN VOGUE.

77

The plastic and metal Flushmate Tank shown here, which will bolt on in place of most porcelain tanks, takes advantage of a home's water pressure (usually 30 to 80 pounds per square inch). As water fills the tank, air is also drawn in through a special valve; the water pressure compresses the air in the tank. When the flush button is depressed, the compressed air forces the water through the bowl with extreme energy.

With this high-pressure tank, conventional bowls that normally require 5 to 7 gallons or more will flush efficiently using only 2 to 2½ gallons. The sudden "ptoosh" of the pressurized flush takes a little getting used to, but it's actually not much louder than a conventional flush—just surprisingly sudden. A plastic cover (available in white and 53 colors) covers up the tank.

Pressurized tank replaces your gravity-feed tank

DOLPHIN BAY
The most exciting waterfront community ever launched at Foster City

UNTIL THIS YEAR, THE FINEST WHIRLPOOL BATHS AVAILABLE DIDN'T EXIST.

THE BOLD LOOK OF KOHLER

WALNUT CREEK, CA.

note MEZZANINES IN THE 2 UPPER INTERIOR VIEWS

new 2-STORY HOMES POPULAR!

CITRUS HTS. CA.   KITCHEN ADJOINS FAMILY ROOM

AMBERWOOD
Pleasanton

From $80,990

Hwy 580 to Santa Rita Road exit. Models located at
4485 Sutter Gate Avenue. (415) 846-7924

'78

GROWING INTEREST IN UNCONVENTIONAL STYLES

WATERFRONT CONDOMINIUMS GROWING IN POPULARITY (BELOW, LEFT and CTR.)

IN VERMONT

TRI-LEVEL

WATSONVILLE, CA.

MEDITERRANEAN *INFLUENCE*
RETURNING — WITH
TILE ROOFS,
HEAVY DOORS, *ETC.*

SAN JOSE, CA.
(EVERGREEN
DIST.)

3-CAR GARAGE

1979 CADILLACS

PEBBLE
BEACH,
CA.

BOYNE
FALLS, MI.

PPG Solarcool® Bronze glass tames the blazing summer sun. And air conditioning costs.

With all of its windows and sliding glass doors glazed with PPG Solarcool Bronze reflective glass, this Sun Belt home looks perfectly beautiful.

A Natural Alternative

Redwood plywood.
Natural, beautiful, affordable.

Boyne Falls LOG HOMES

TRADITIONAL
STYLES
ALSO
CONTINUE.

79

NATURAL WOOD HOMES

SEATTLE

CORAL
GABLES, FL.

PPG INDUSTRIES

DOUBLE-PANED
and
TINTED GLASS
WINDOWS
POPULAR IN
MANY REGIONS.

SPANISH-STYLE
ARCHED
ENTRY TO
PATIO

WATSONVILLE, CA.

ATLANTA, GA.

HOT TUB

WHIRLPOOL HOT TUBS A NOVELTY, and TRENDY!

©AMERICAN-STANDARD
World's leading name in plumbing fixtures and fittings
Soaking Tub with whirlpool.

BATHROOM IN NATURAL WOOD WITH SKYLIGHT

It takes an international leader like American-Standard to combine this kind of European design excellence with the American preference for versatility. We start with the Tilche Suite, designed by Paolo Tilche, recognized as one of Europe's leading designers. Every curve, every line painstakingly defined to complement the design. But greater beauty lies in its adaptability, translating into bathrooms that reflect your style… your lifestyle. We can only begin to show you the possibilities. Oriental. Contemporary. Early American. The Tilche Suite. It inspires endless decors beautifully interpreted with American flair.

79

Water-saving engineering, pioneered by American-Standard in 1965, available on selected models. The exclusive Vent-Away, with fingertip control for removal of odors.

WATERLESS COMPOSTING COMMODE

HOW TOILET IS VENTED — VENT PIPE
COMMODE
AIR FLOW
INNER CONTAINER
OUTER CONTAINER

The Tilche Suite from the American-Standard International Group.

AVAIL. SINCE MID~ 1978

Everything about this bathroom says "Now!" The uncluttered lines of the Tilche Suite. The fashionable color choice, Americana Brown, for all fixtures including the luxurious oval Ultra Bath. Noteworthy, the elegance of American-Standard 24 karat gold plated fittings.

The Tilche Suite. Curves and angles make it a pleasure to look at. Shown here in new Aegean Mist with a 24-karat gold plated Ultra Font faucet. The 22" x 21" sculptured pedestal lavatory and unique toilet are available in a wide range of decorator colors.

AM.~STD.

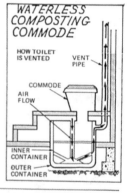

ELJER

ELJER "GALLERY COLLECTION" IN "ELJER COCOA" COLOR

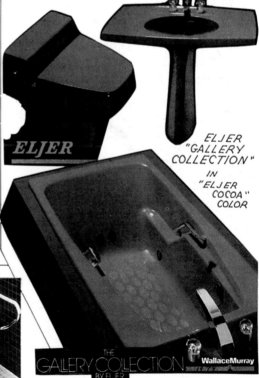

THE GALLERY COLLECTION BY ELJER   WallaceMurray

Luxor Toilet. Shown in Bone.

AMERICAN~STD.
New Lexington Toilet. Shown in Americana Brown.

KOHLER

new HIGH~UP W.C. WITH INVALID ASSIST BARS →

OLD STYLES BEING REVIVED IN THE 1980s!

NEO~TUDOR

Introducing Pella's Contemporary French Sliding Glass Door...

New

WALNUT CREEK, CA.

SACRAMENTO, CA.

SOLAR HOMES

Elder Creek Village

- Domestic Solar Hot Water System
- Full Solar System - Optional
- Thermal pane Windows
- Jenn-air Range with Self-cleaning Oven

80

WINDMILL FARMS

COTATI, CA.

At $59,950 The Price is Right!

SOLAR HOMES

IRON BANNISTERS IN STYLE

A RENEWED INTEREST IN ART DECO GLASS BLOCKS!

GLASS BLOCK SHOWER STALL

Modular Homes

The Affordable Alternative

Jotul, the ultimate in woodstoves

introduces The Elg™

TOWNHOMES

Kitchen

FLUORESCENT LIGHTS ABOVE CEILING

CONDOMINIUMS

DISCOVER ATHENA:
The home improvement that improves your mood every time you use it.

Jacuzzi WHIRLPOOL BATH